MASTERPEACE MANDALAS

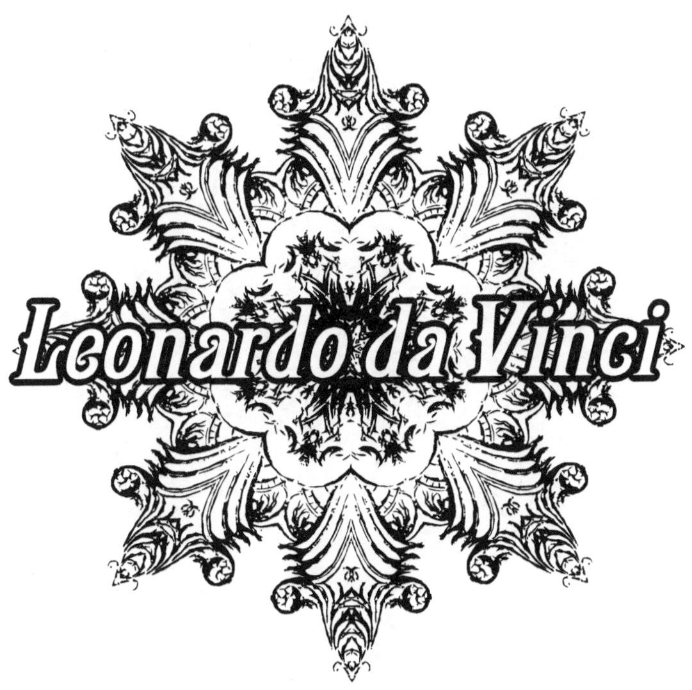

DaVINCI Coloring Book VOLUME 1

This book does not recommend, promote or advise any diagnosis or treatment for any condition and is not a substitute for qualified professional consultation. But it could be fun.

ISBN-10: 1944381007
ISBN-13: 978-1-944381-00-4

Da Vinci Masterpeace Mandalas
Coloring Book
Volume 1

Stop by and tell us what you think
www.masterpeacebooks.com

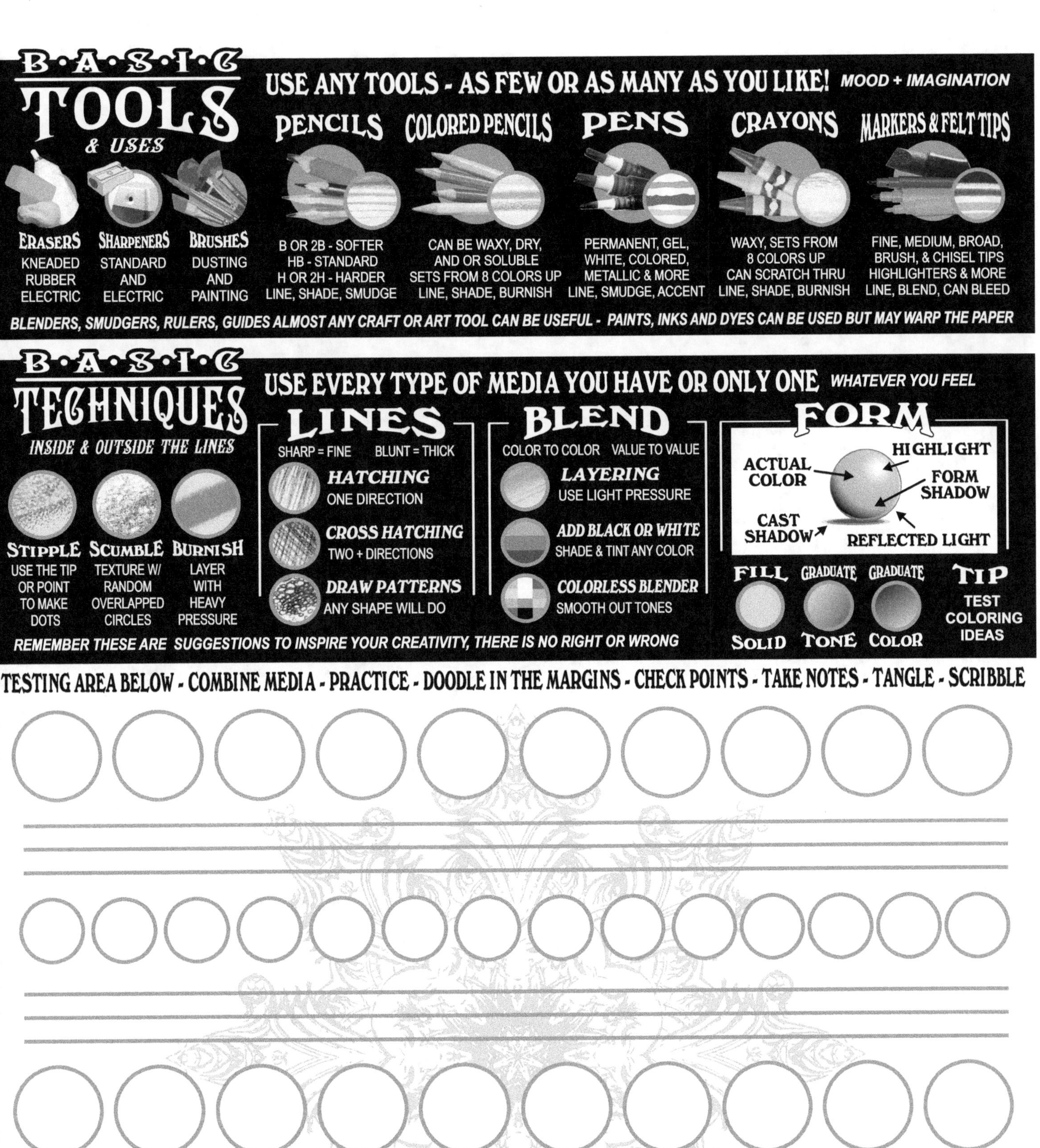

REMEMBER THERE IS NO RIGHT OR WRONG WAY TO COLOR - COLOR HOW YOU FEEL - WHEN YOU FEEL - AND AS LONG AS YOU FEEL

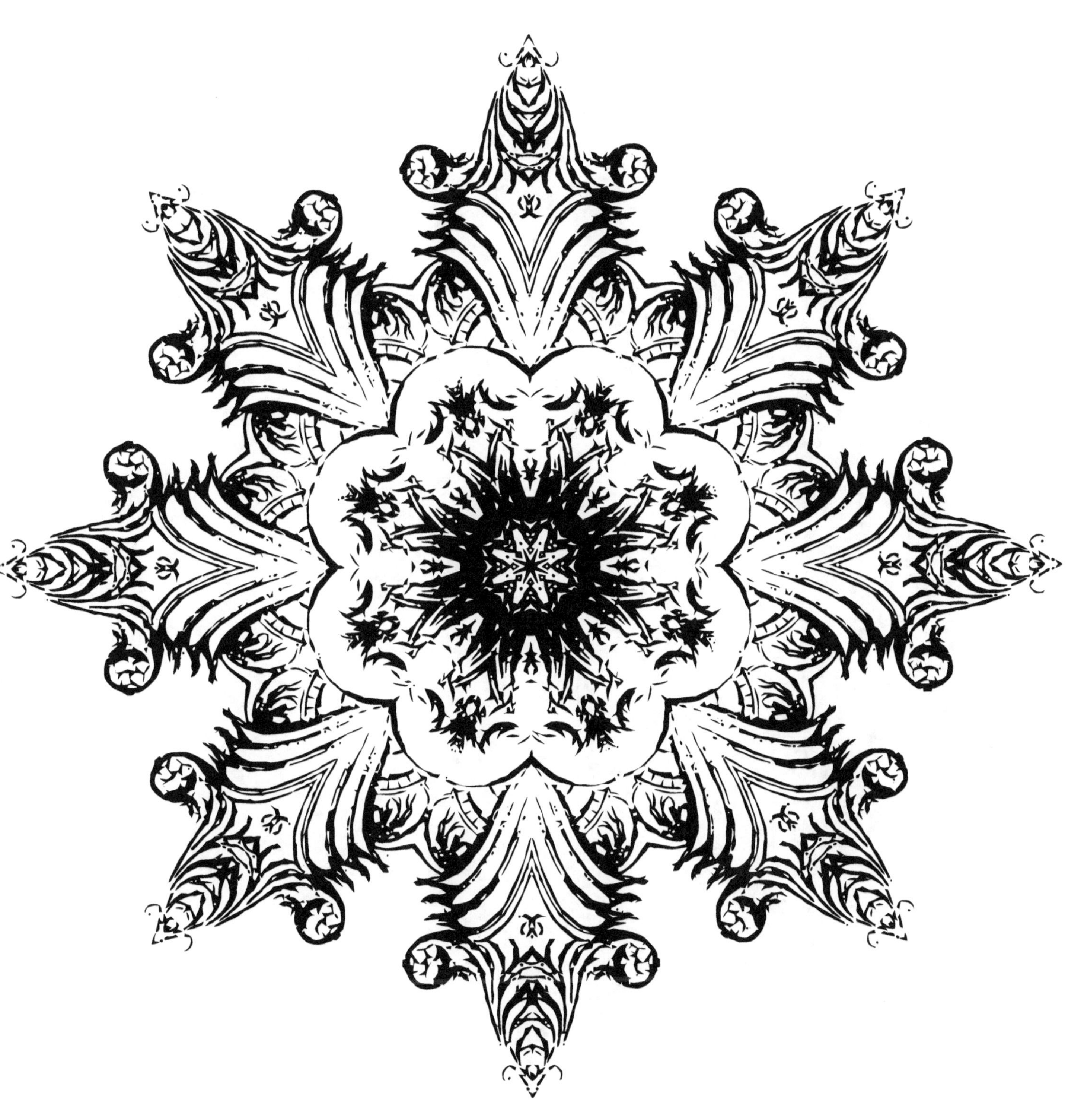

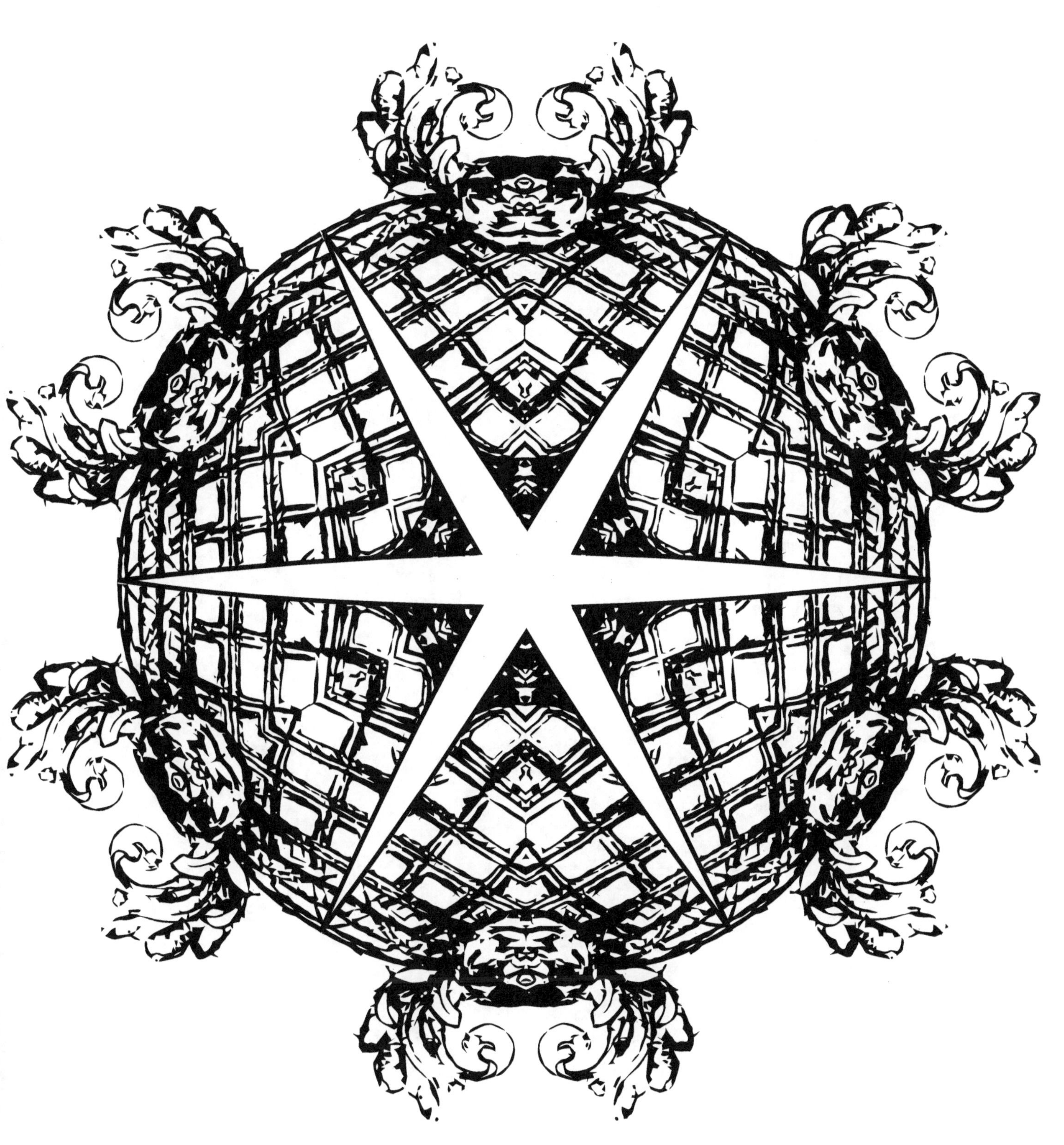

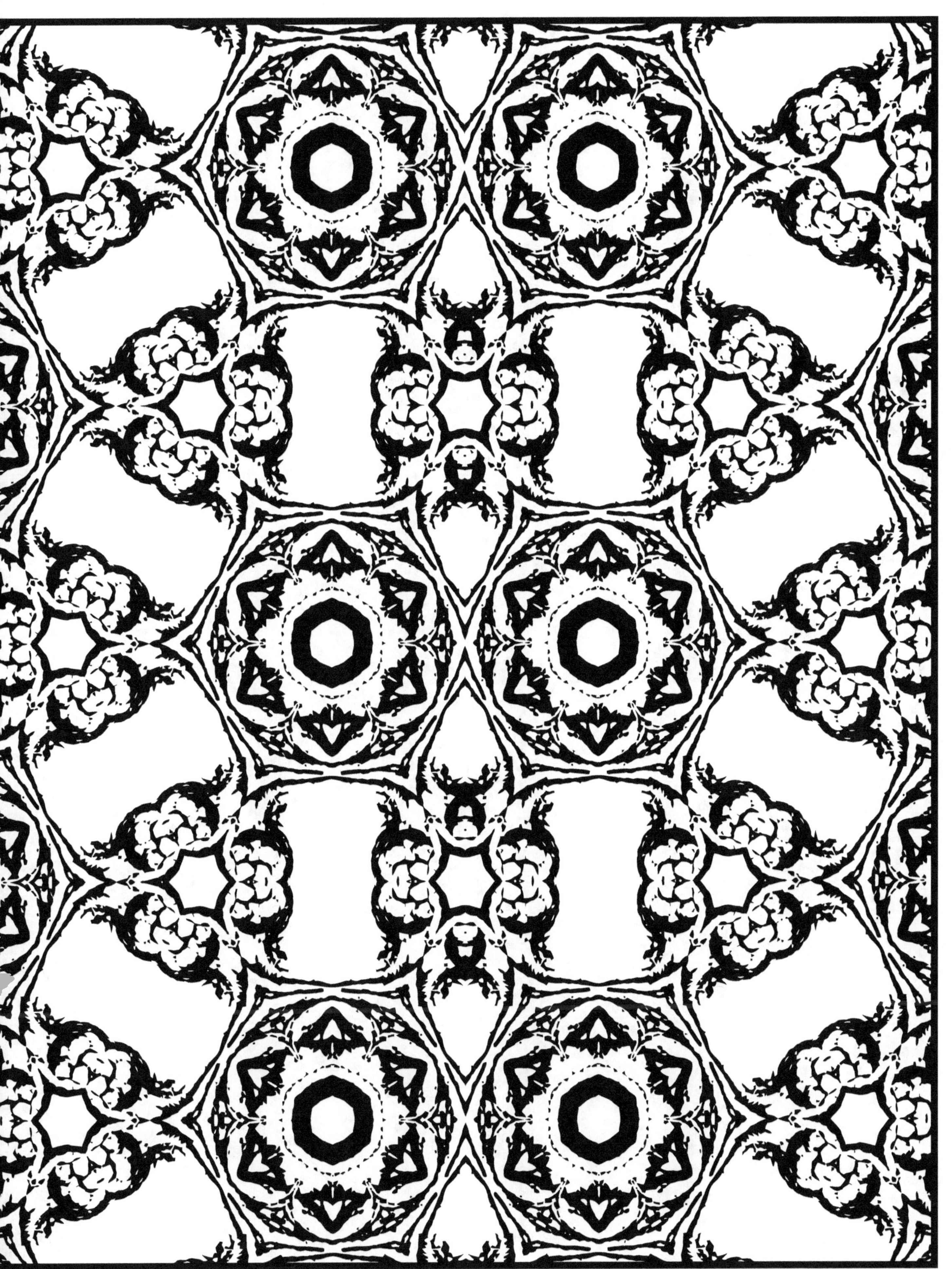

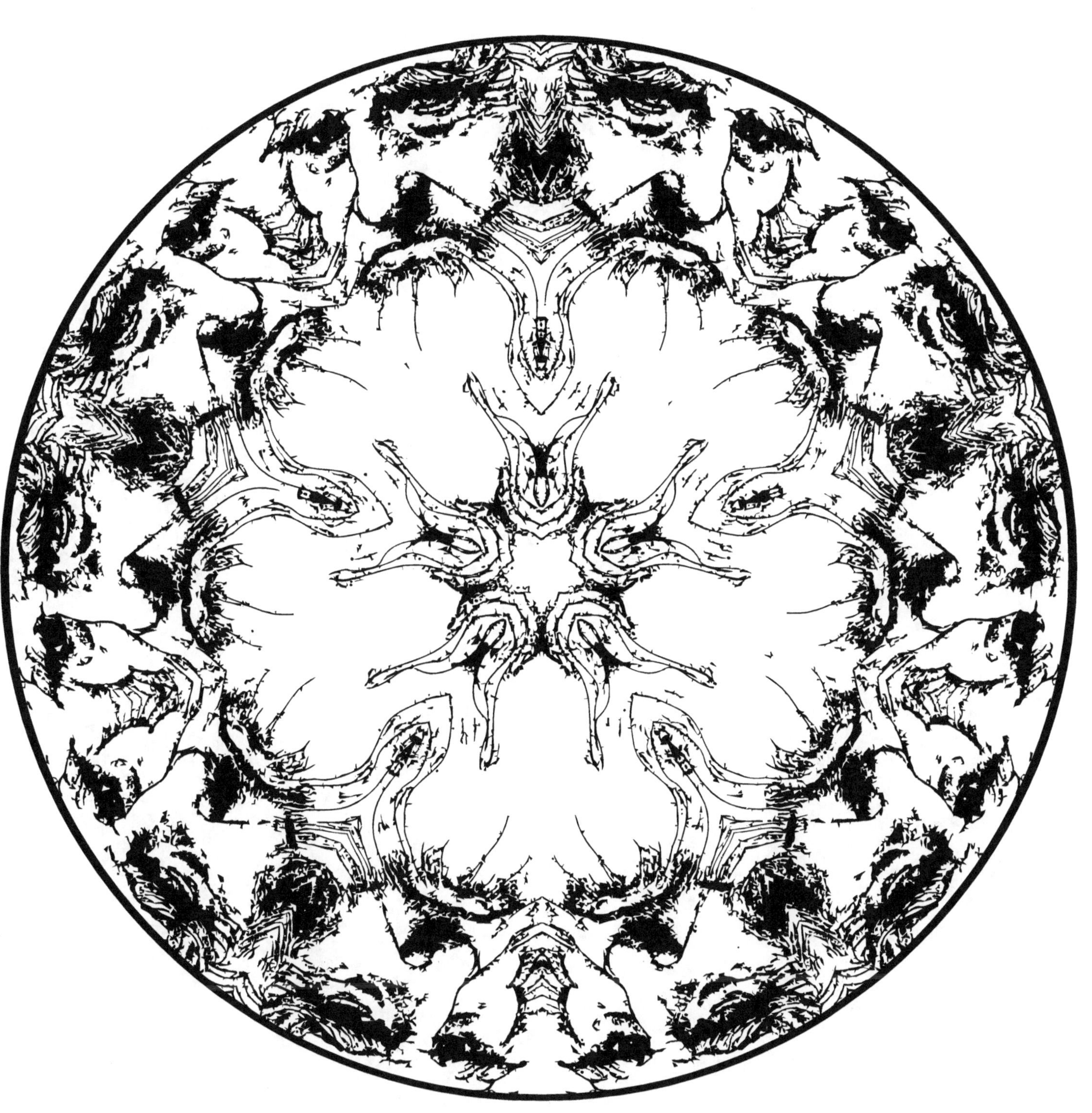

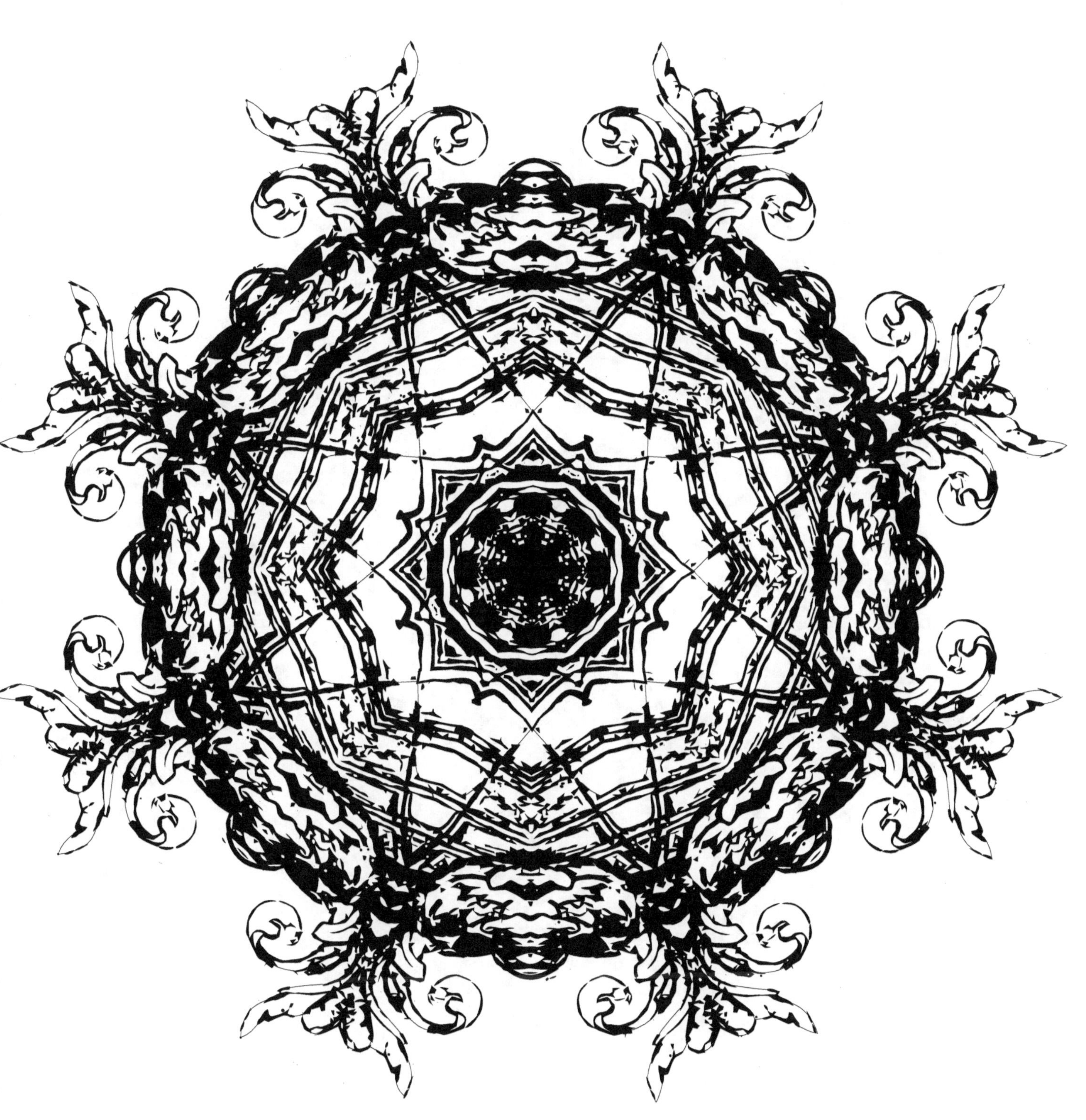

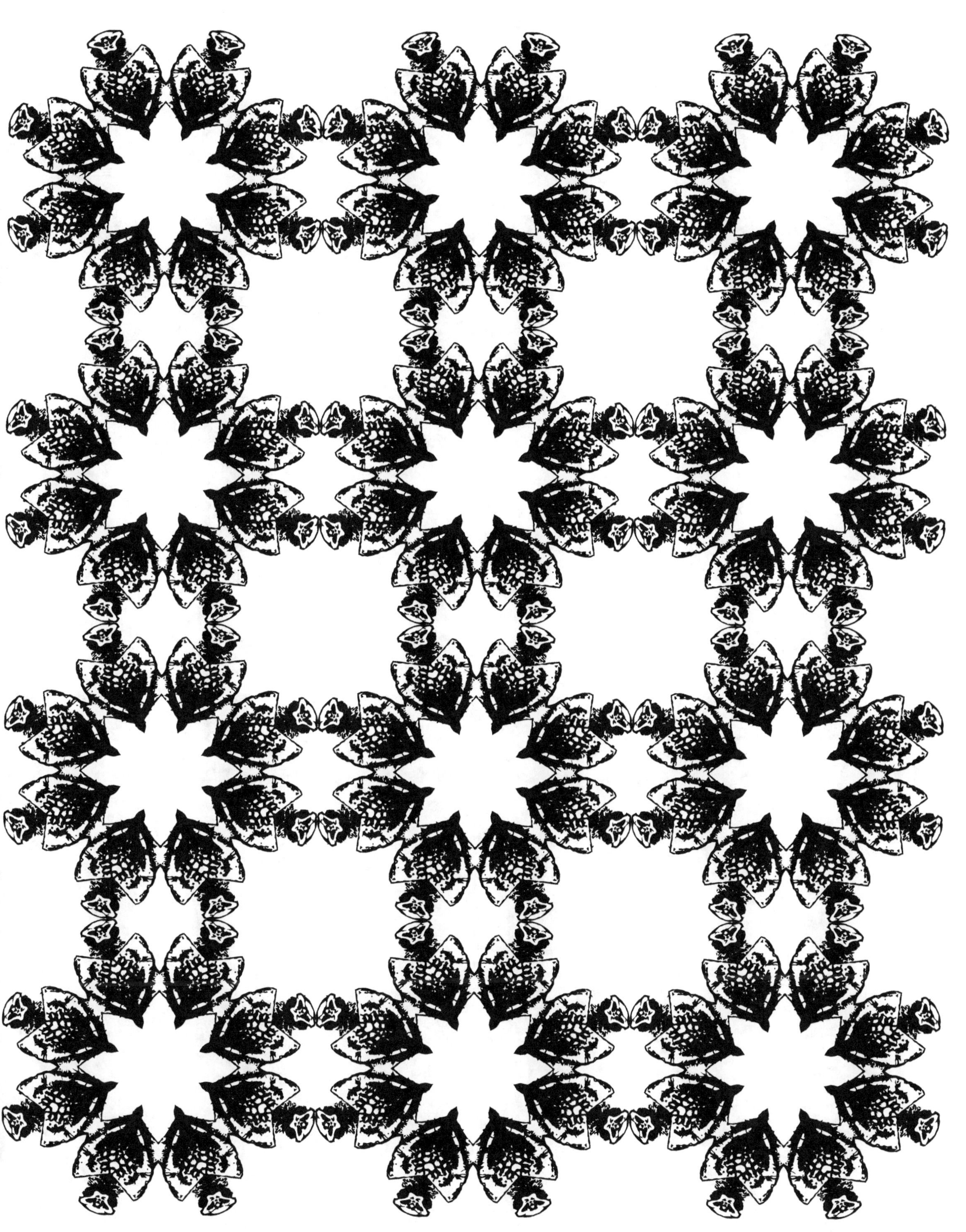

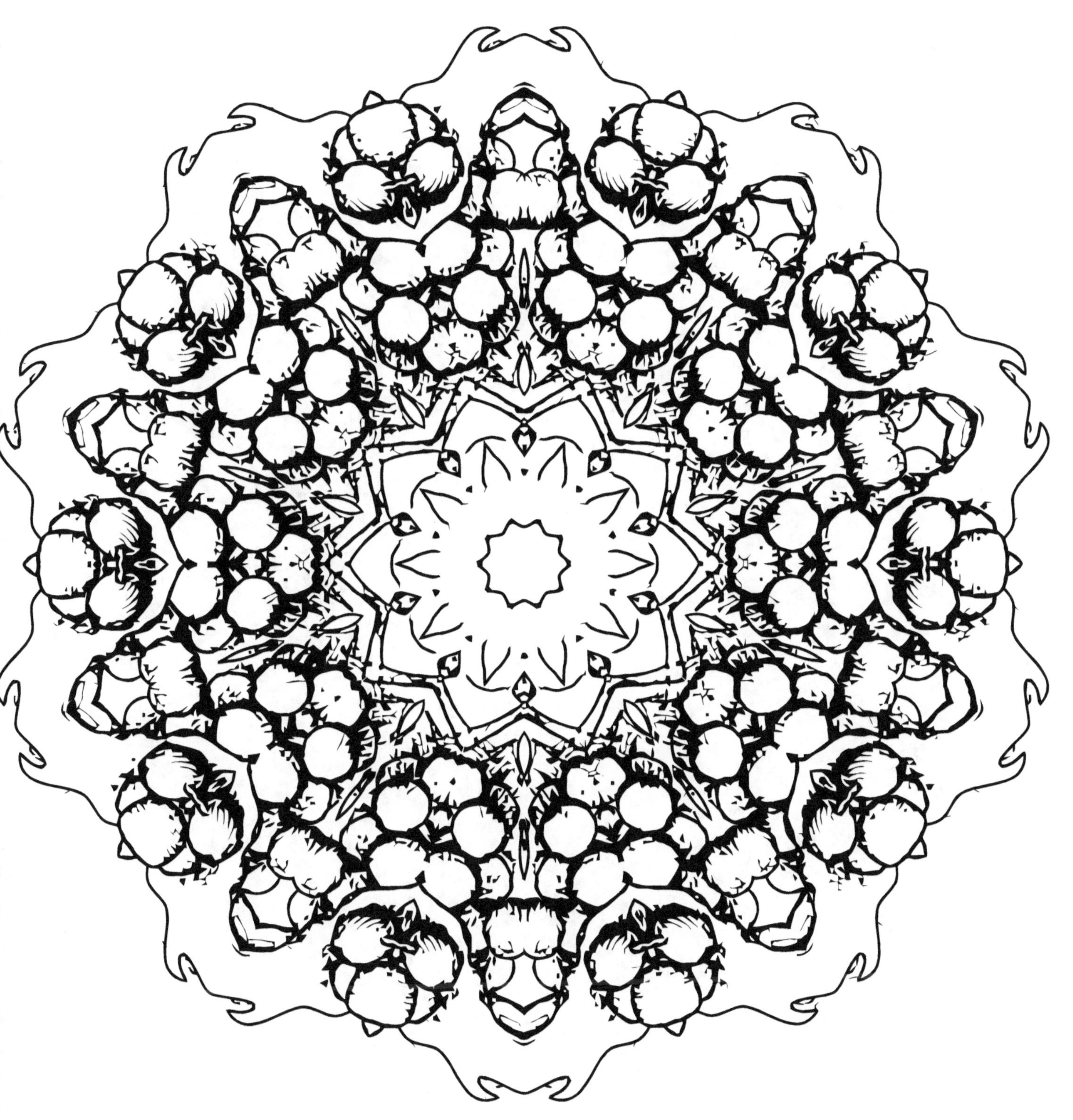

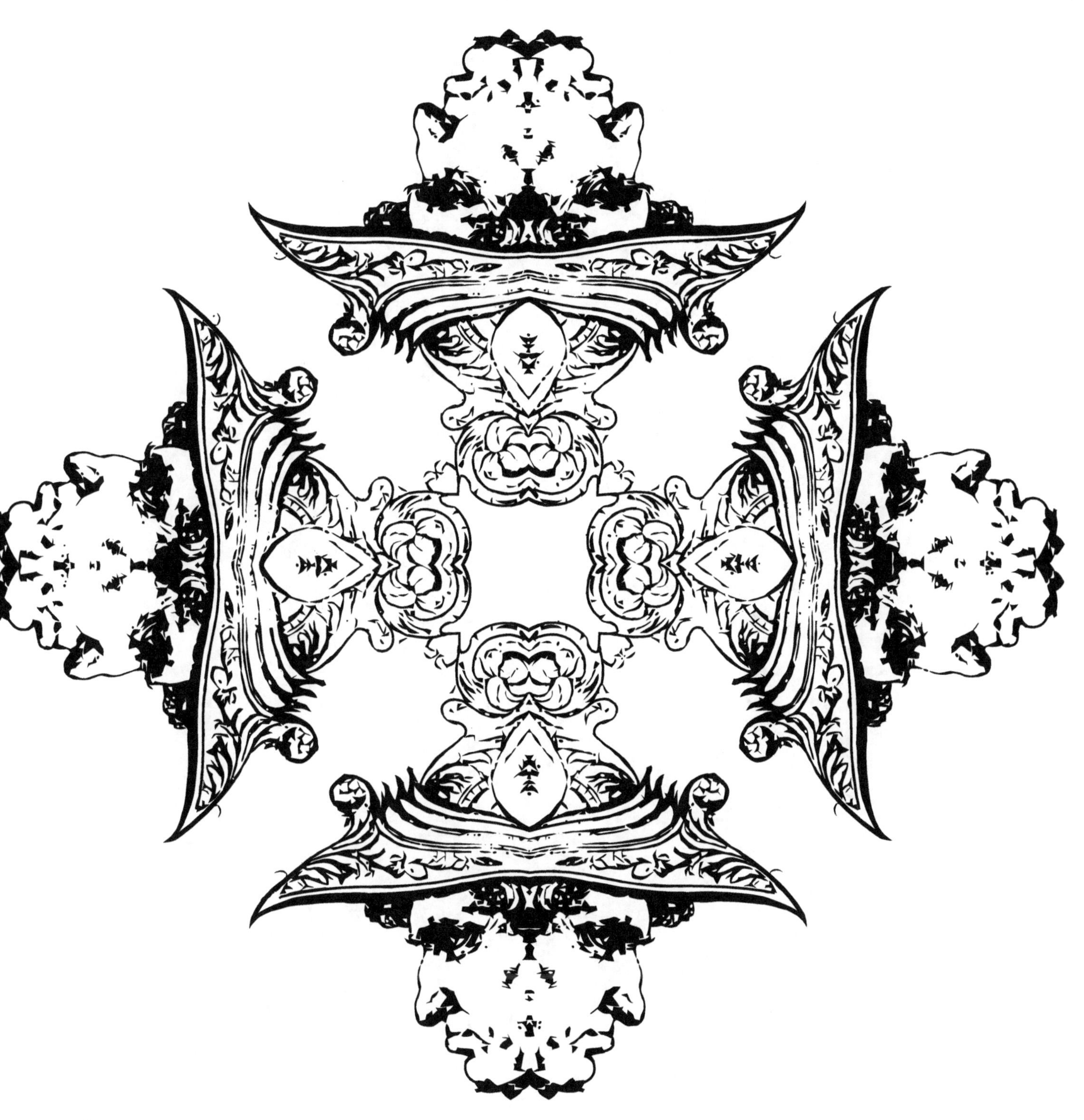

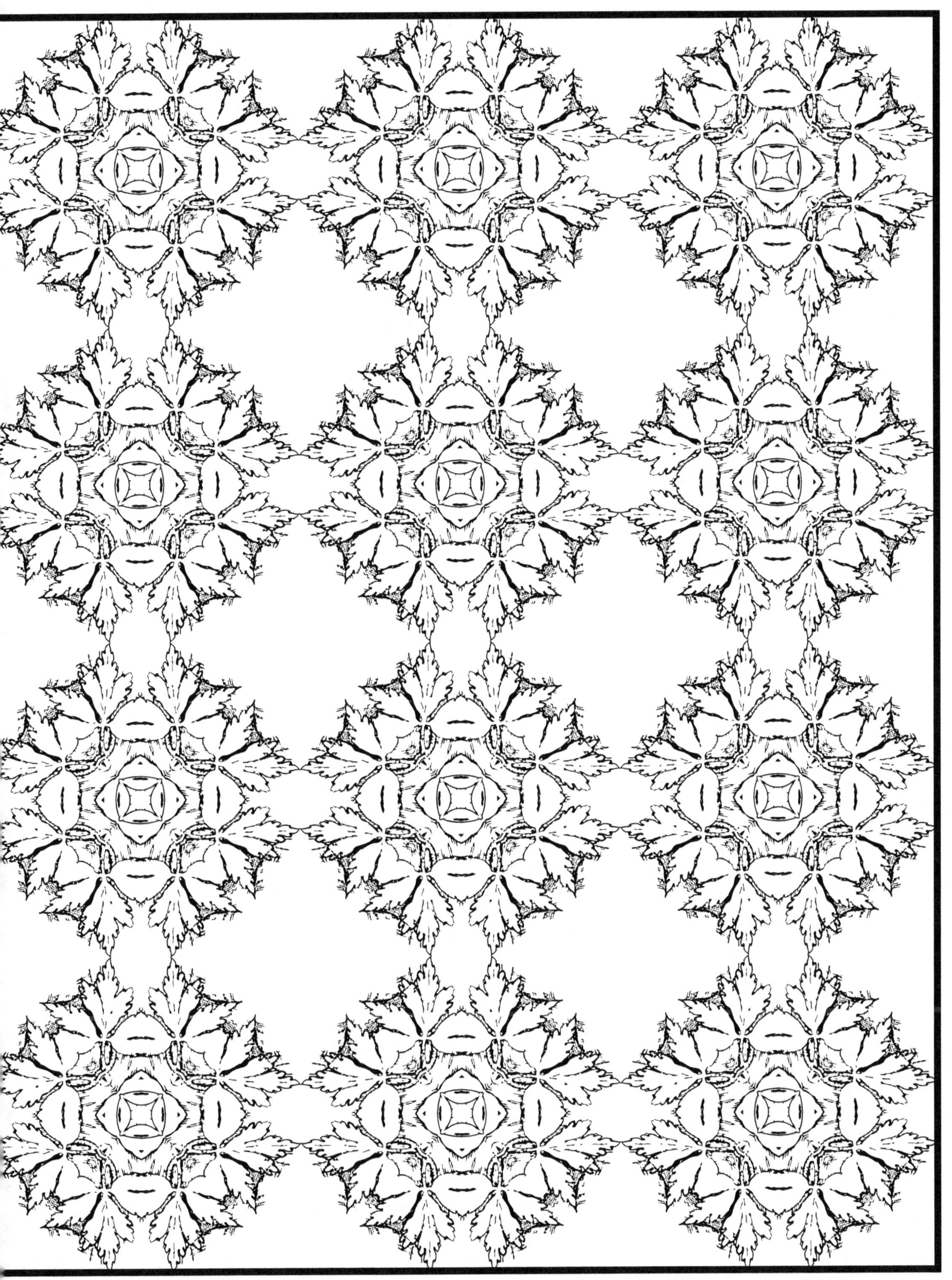

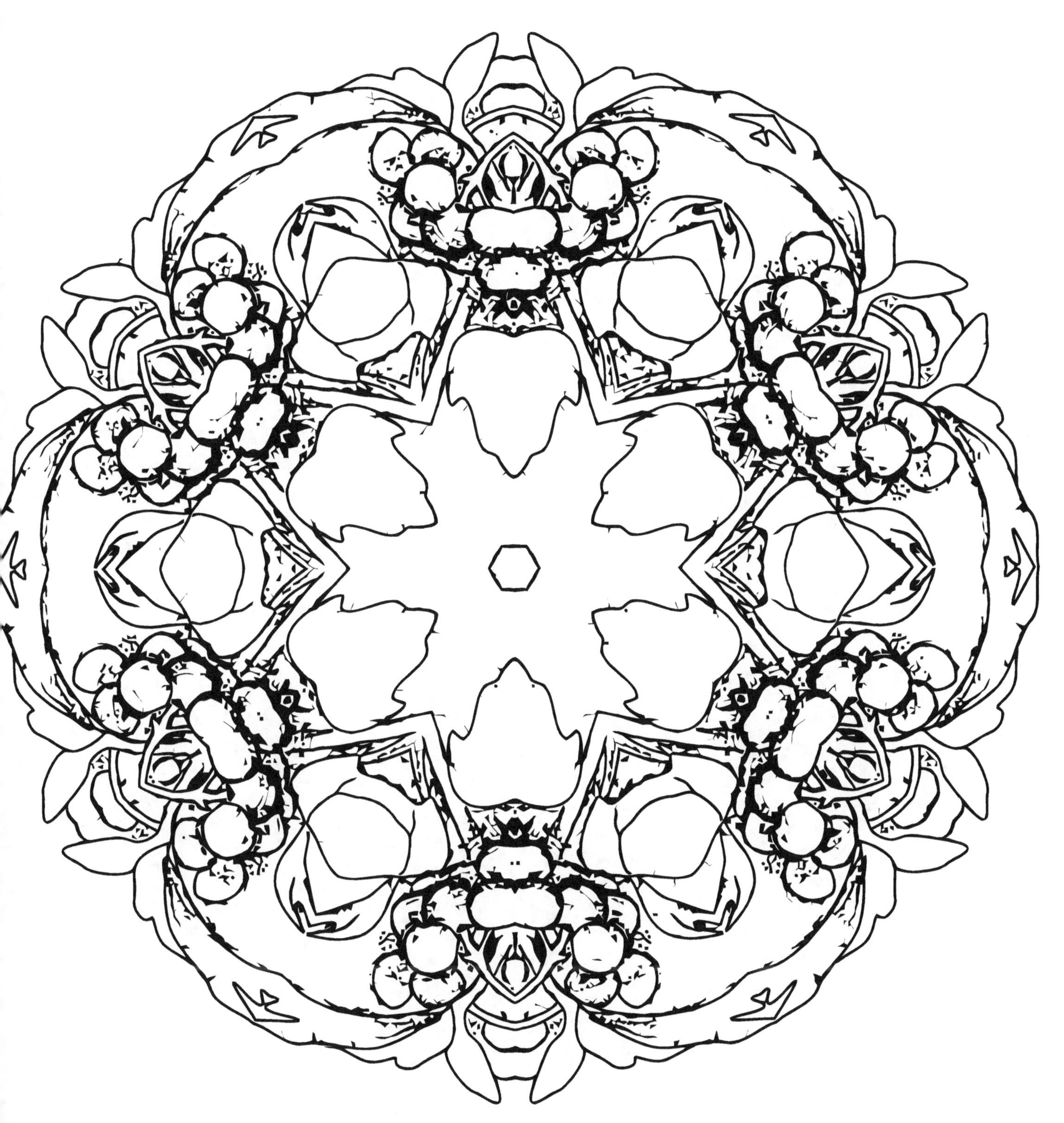

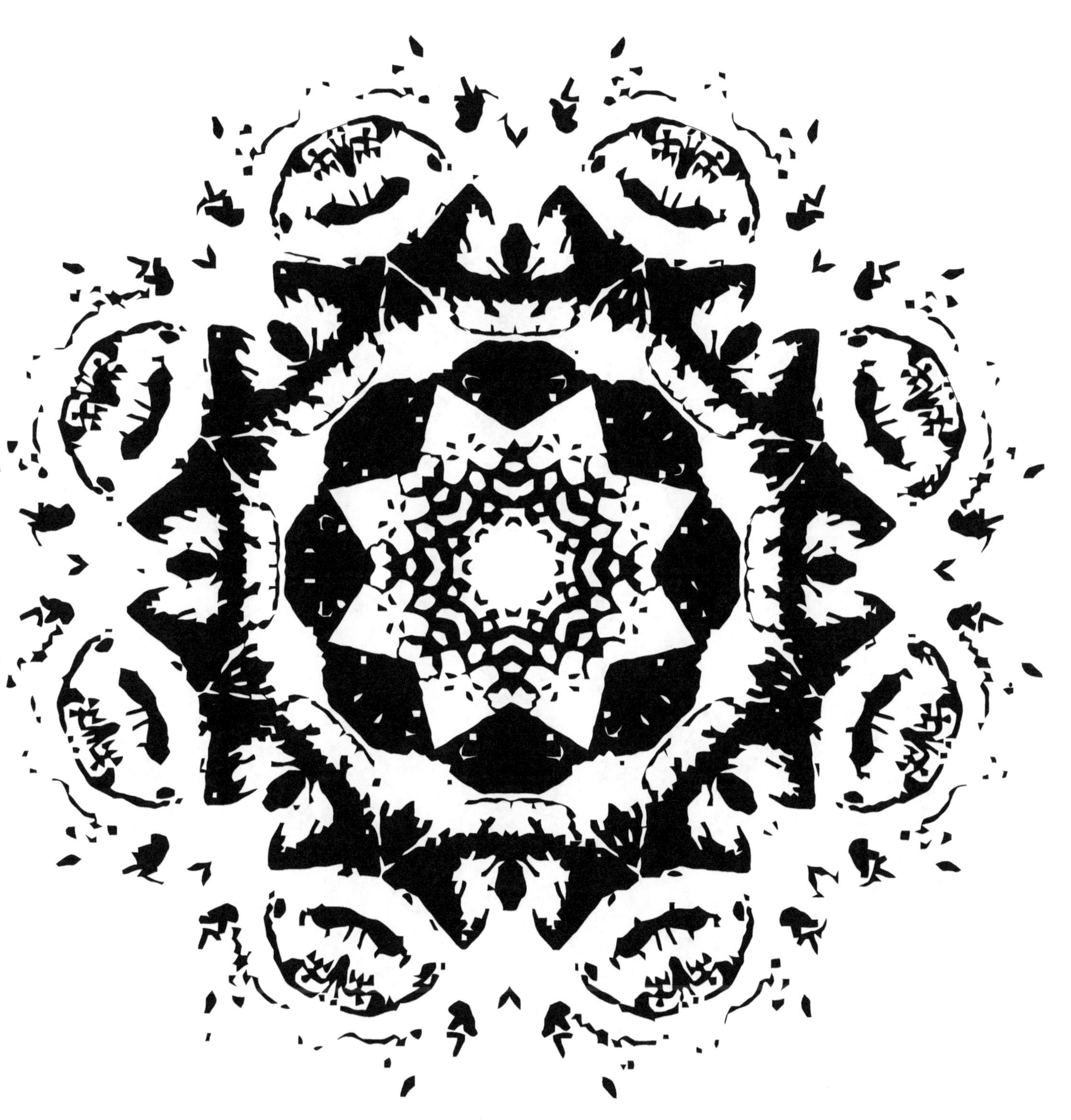

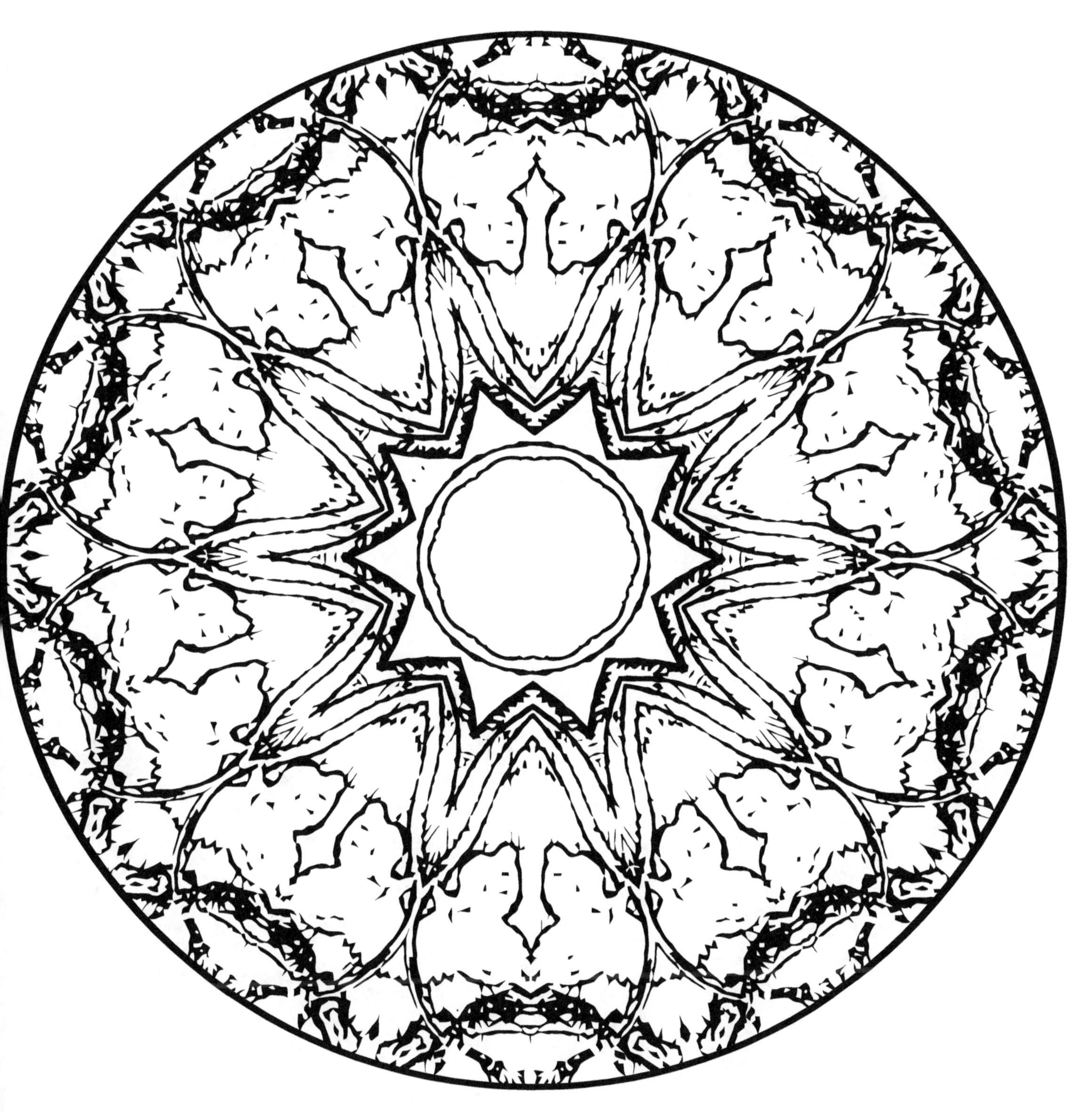

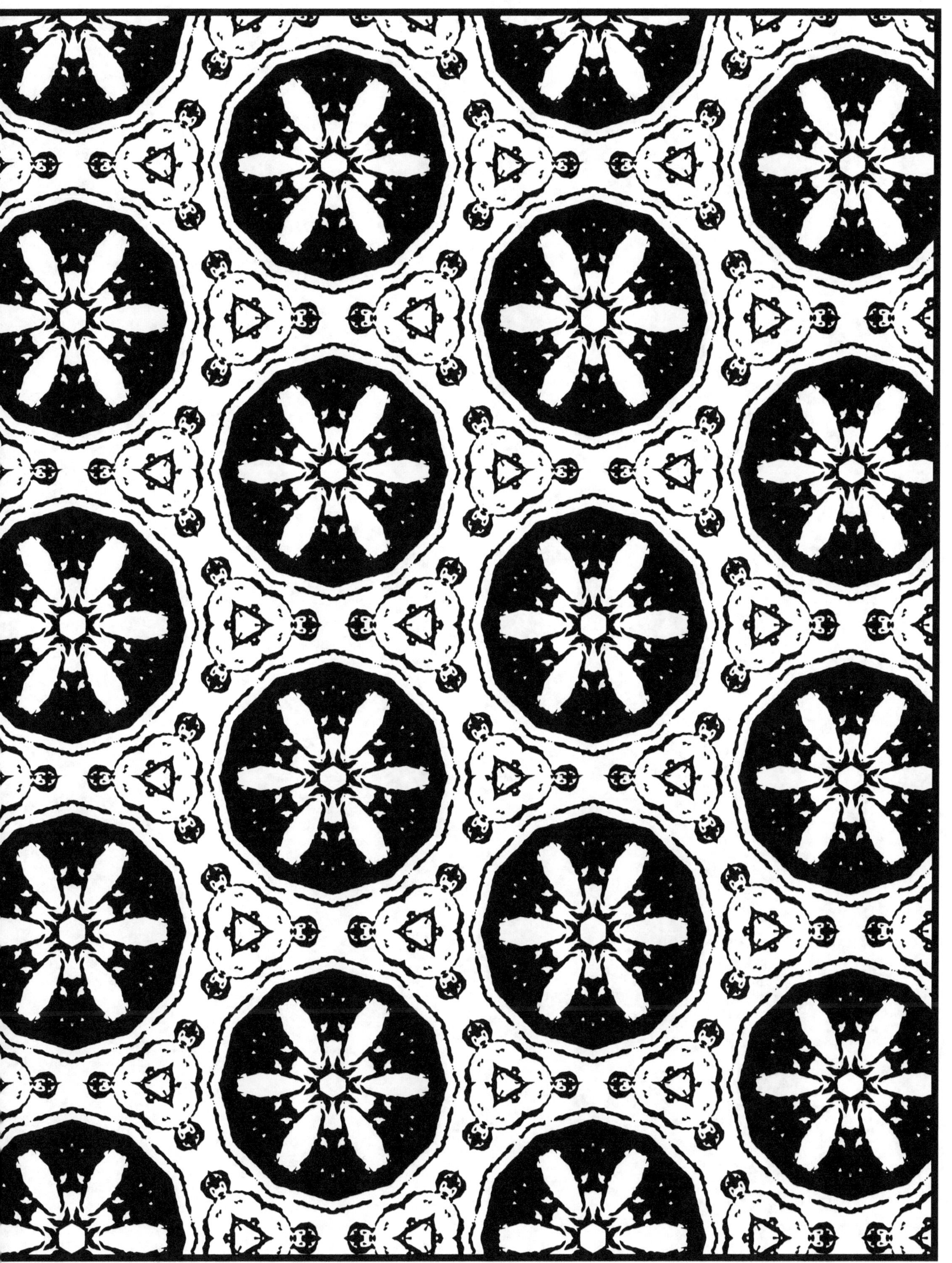

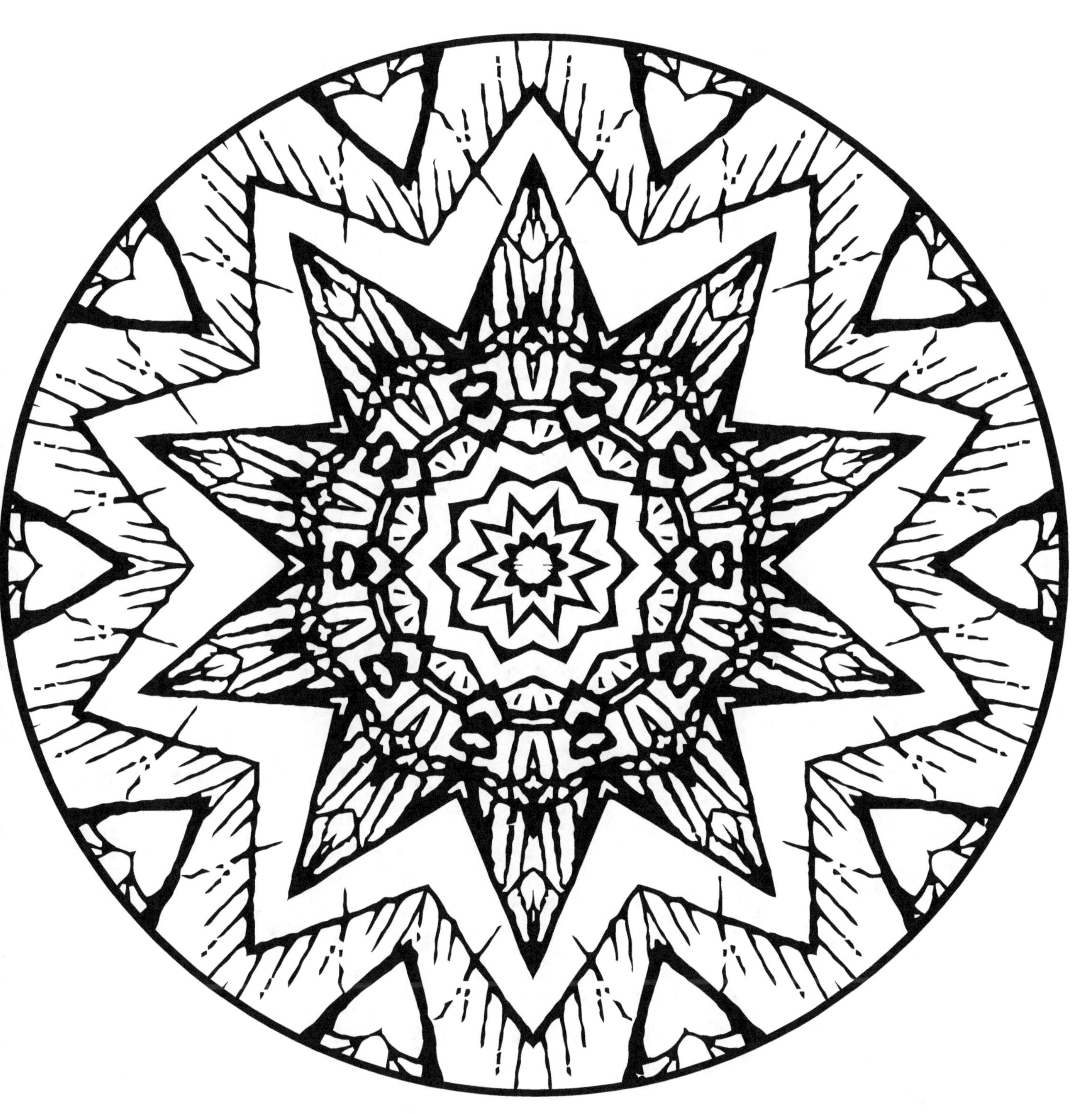

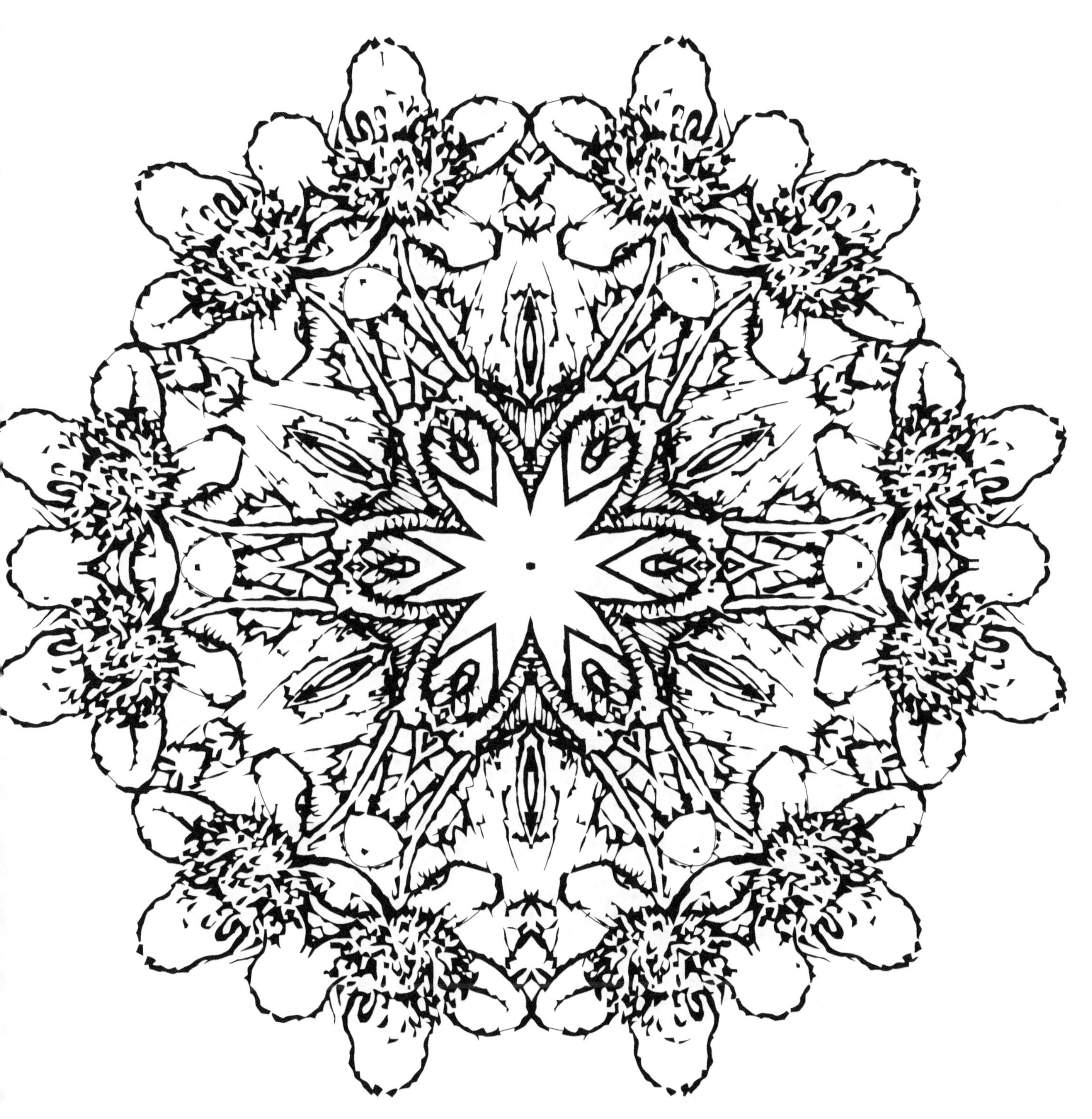

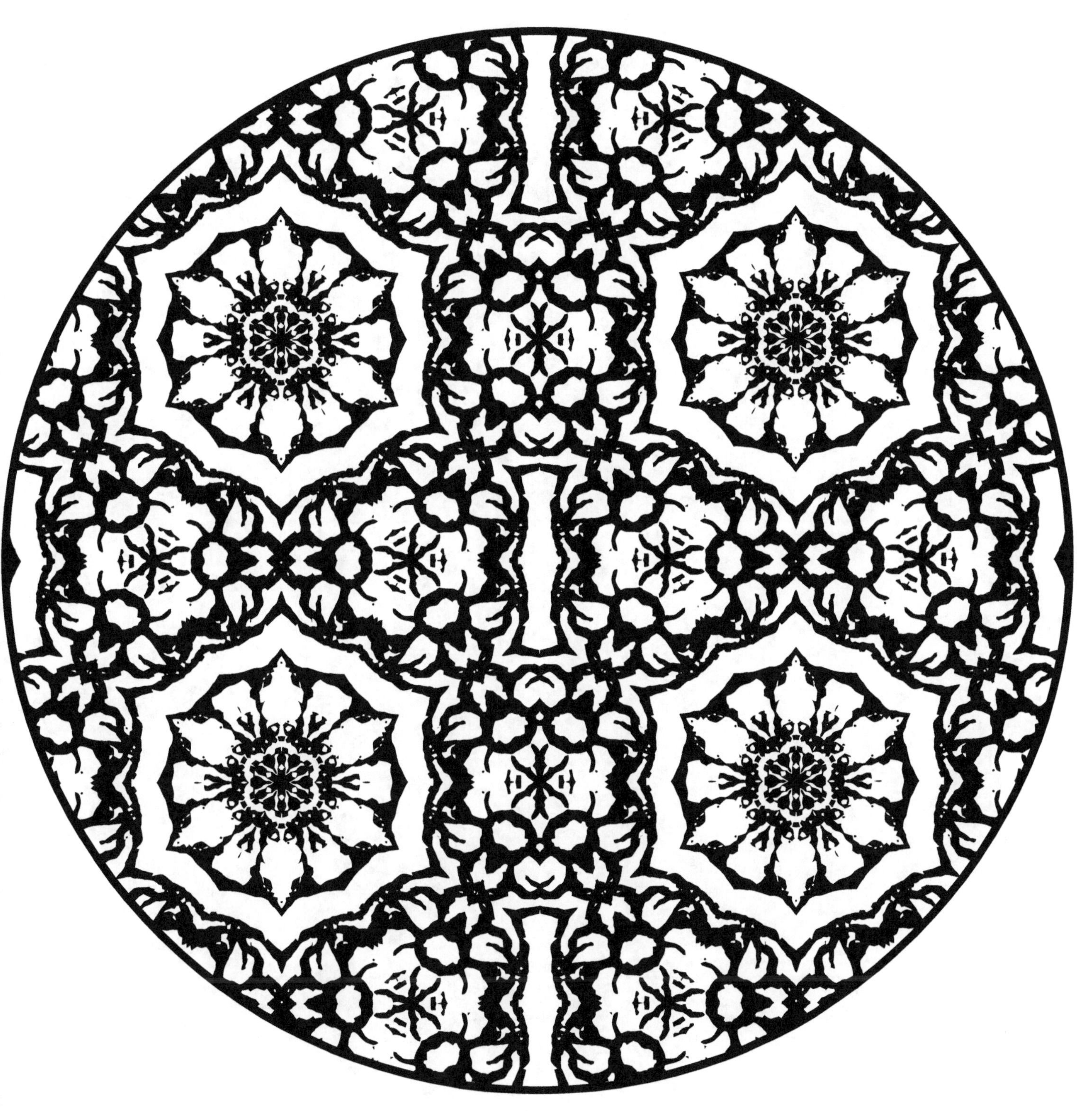

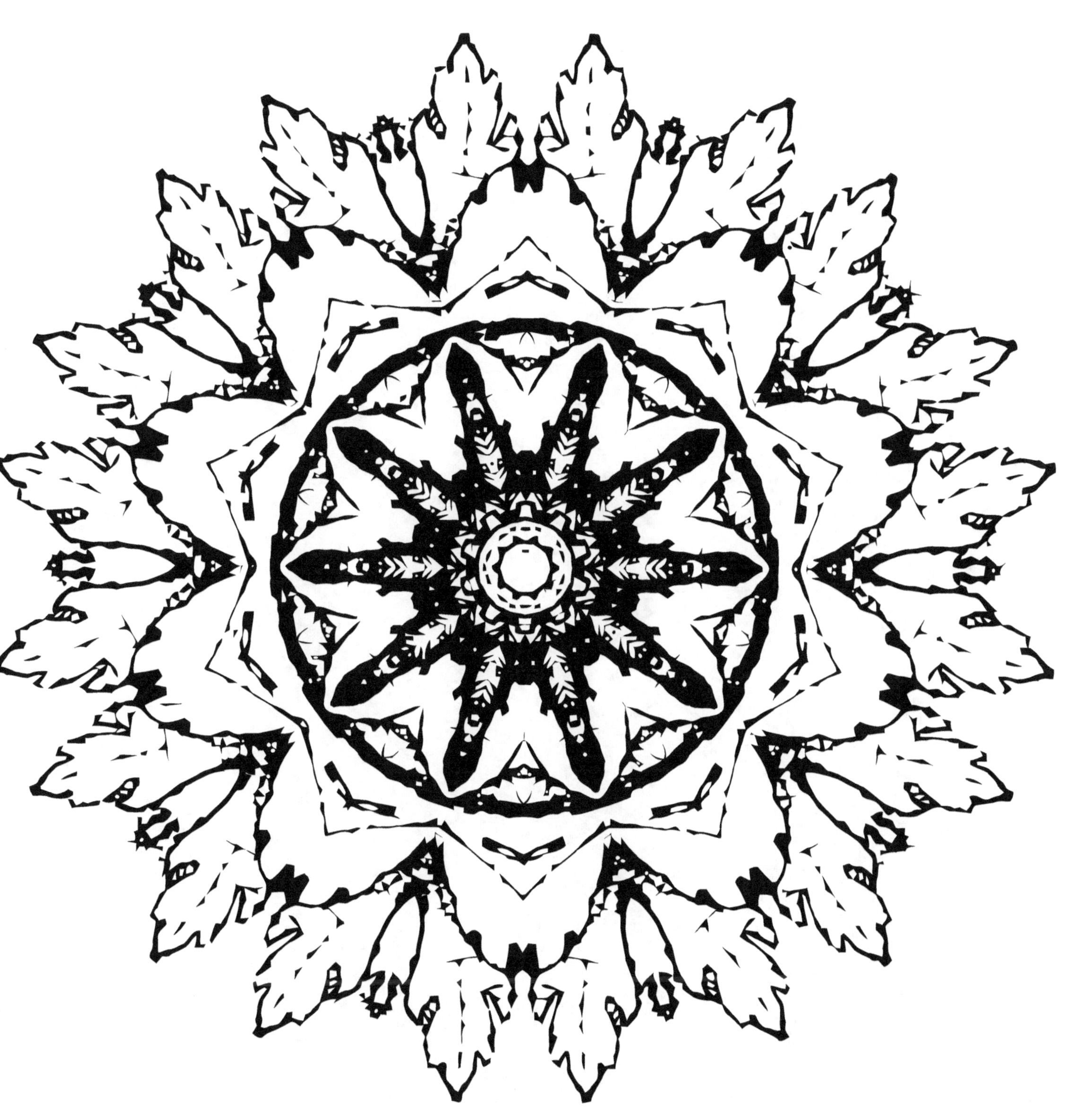

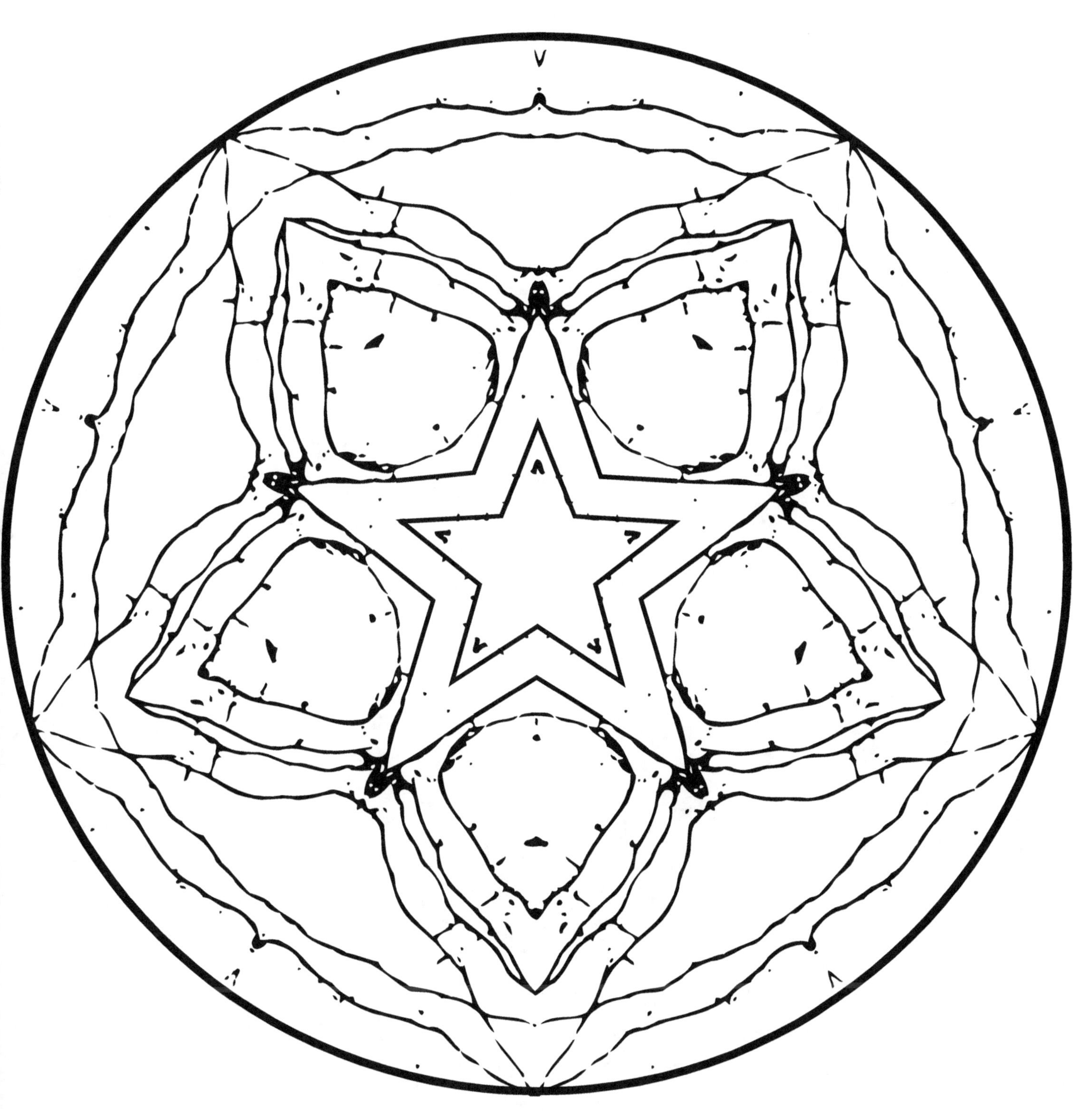

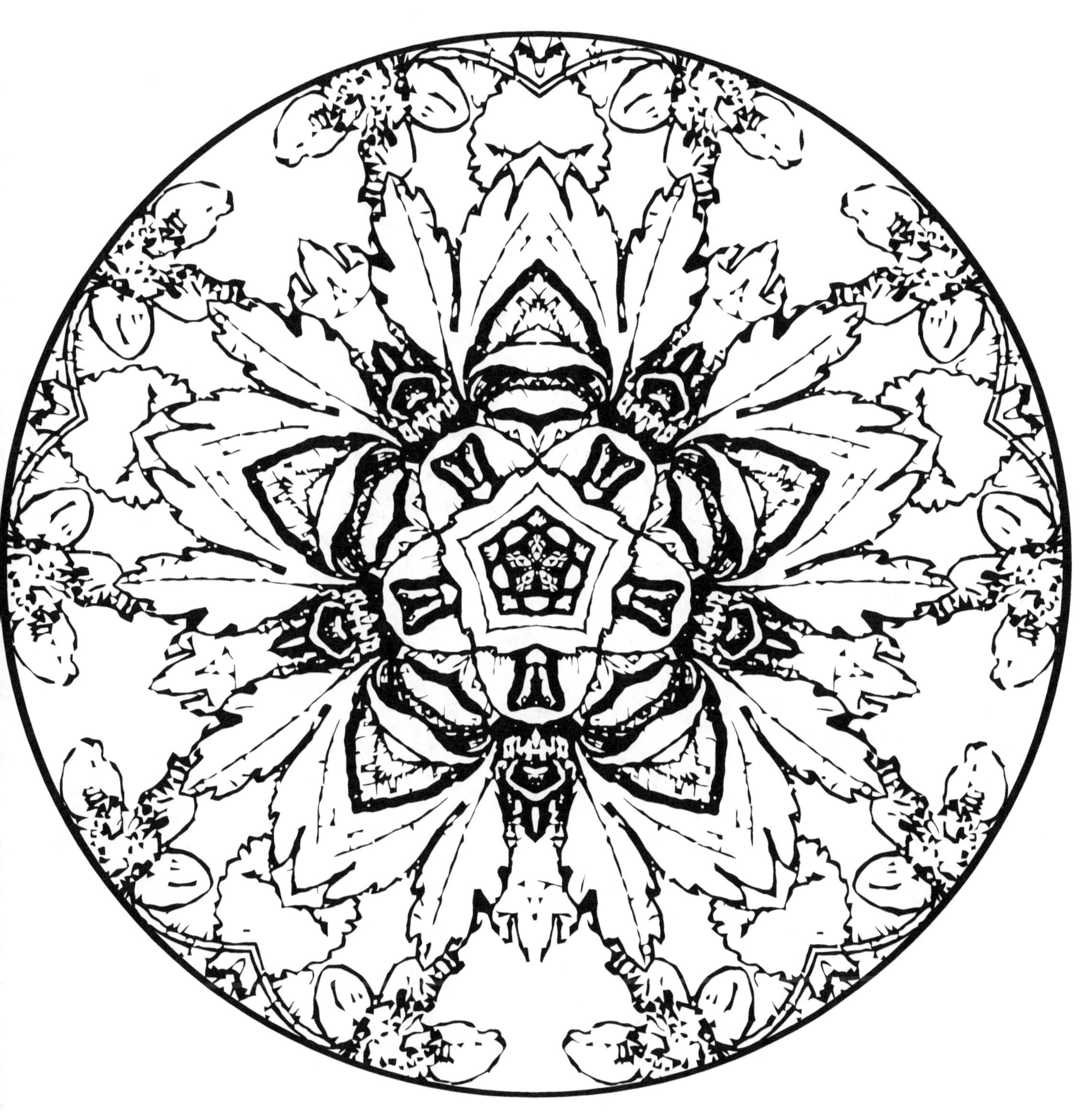

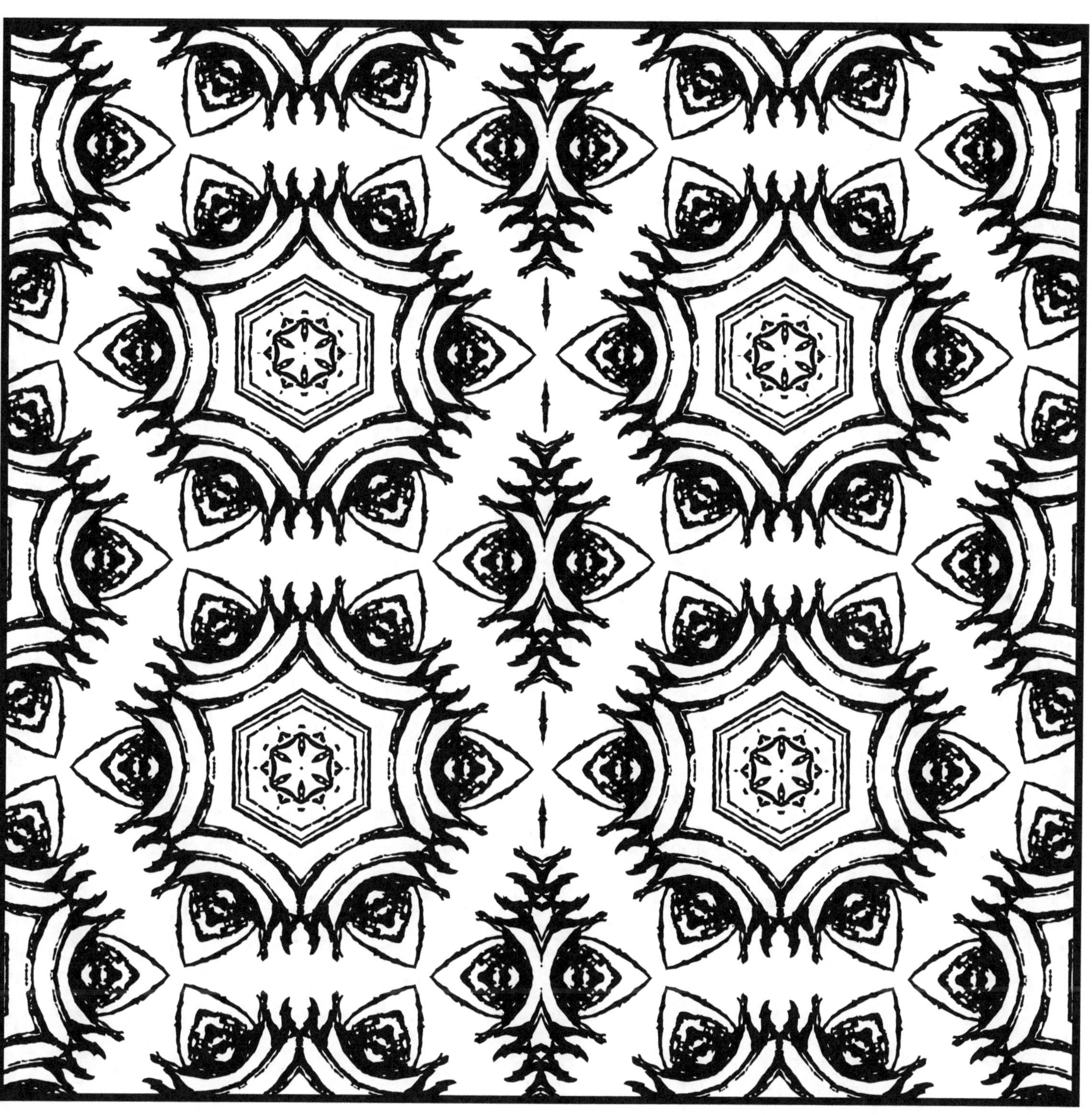

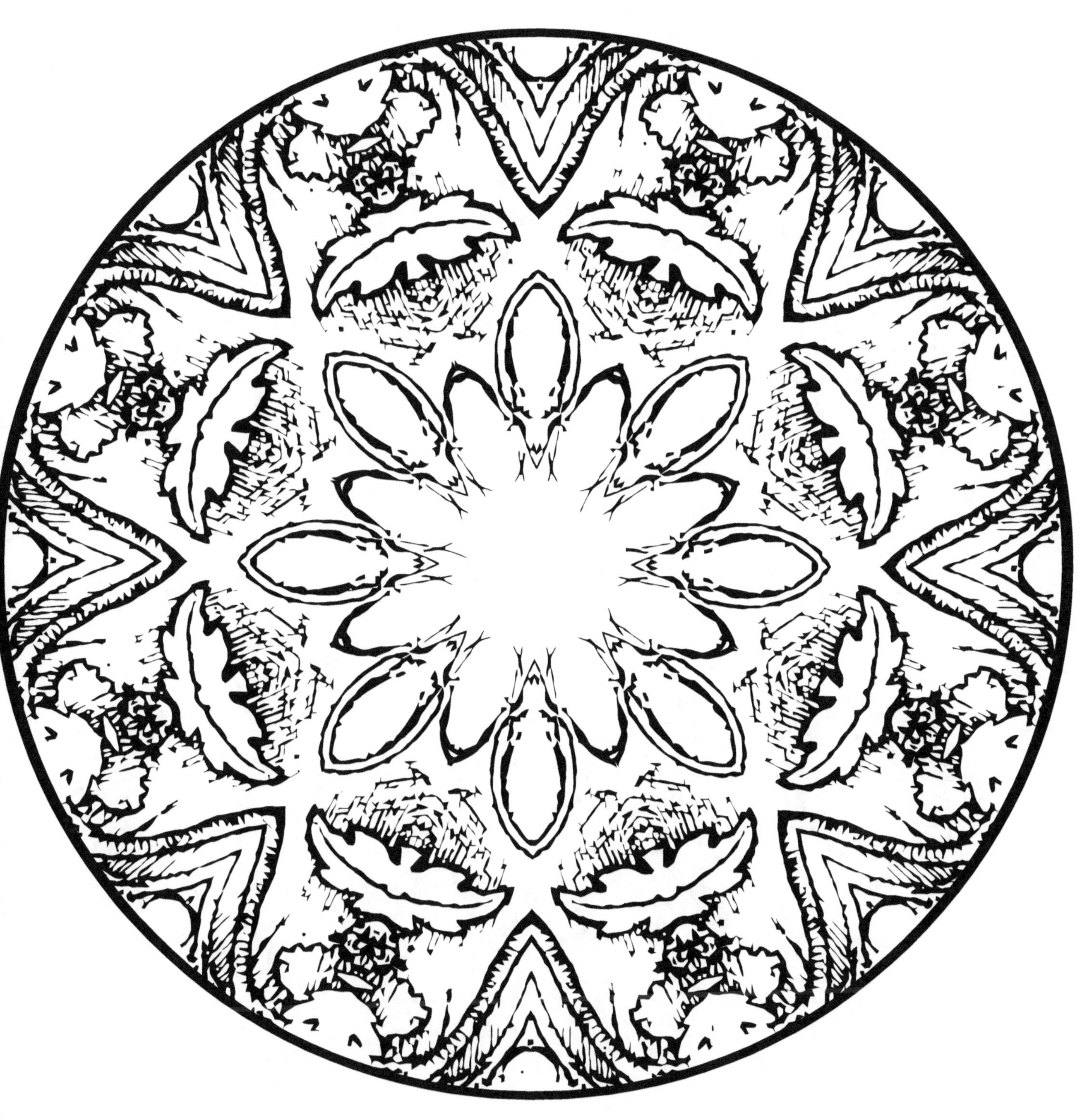

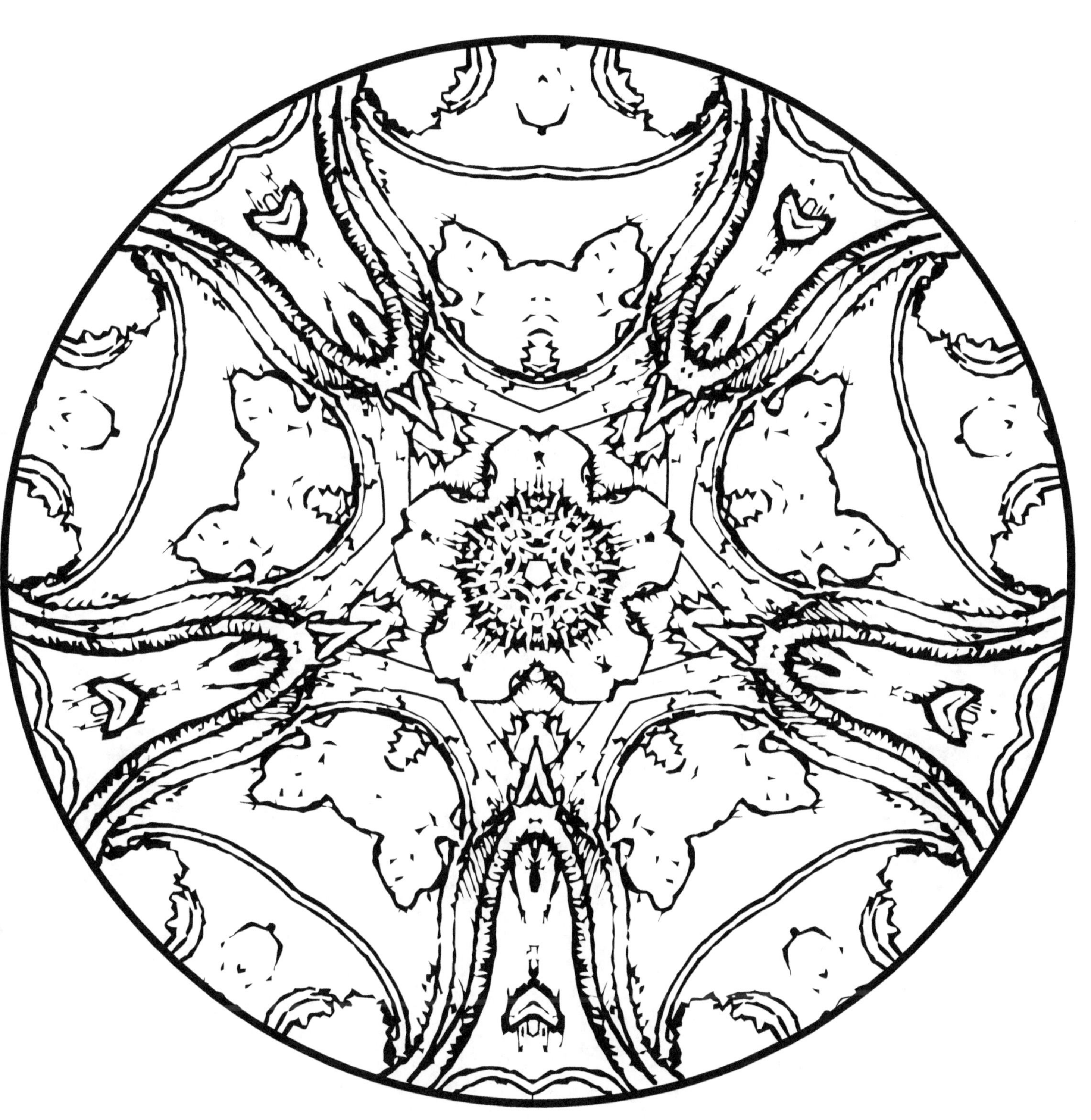

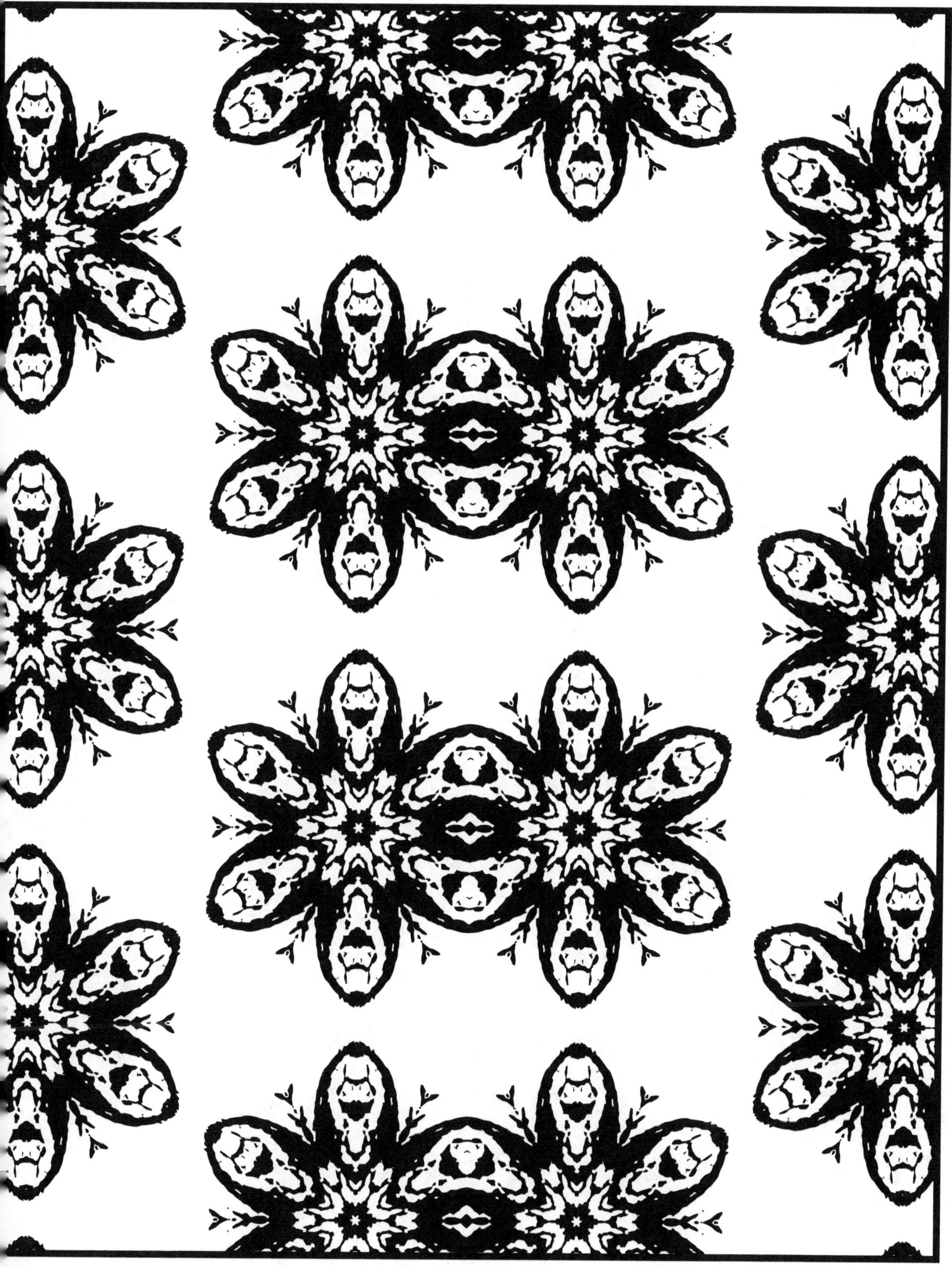

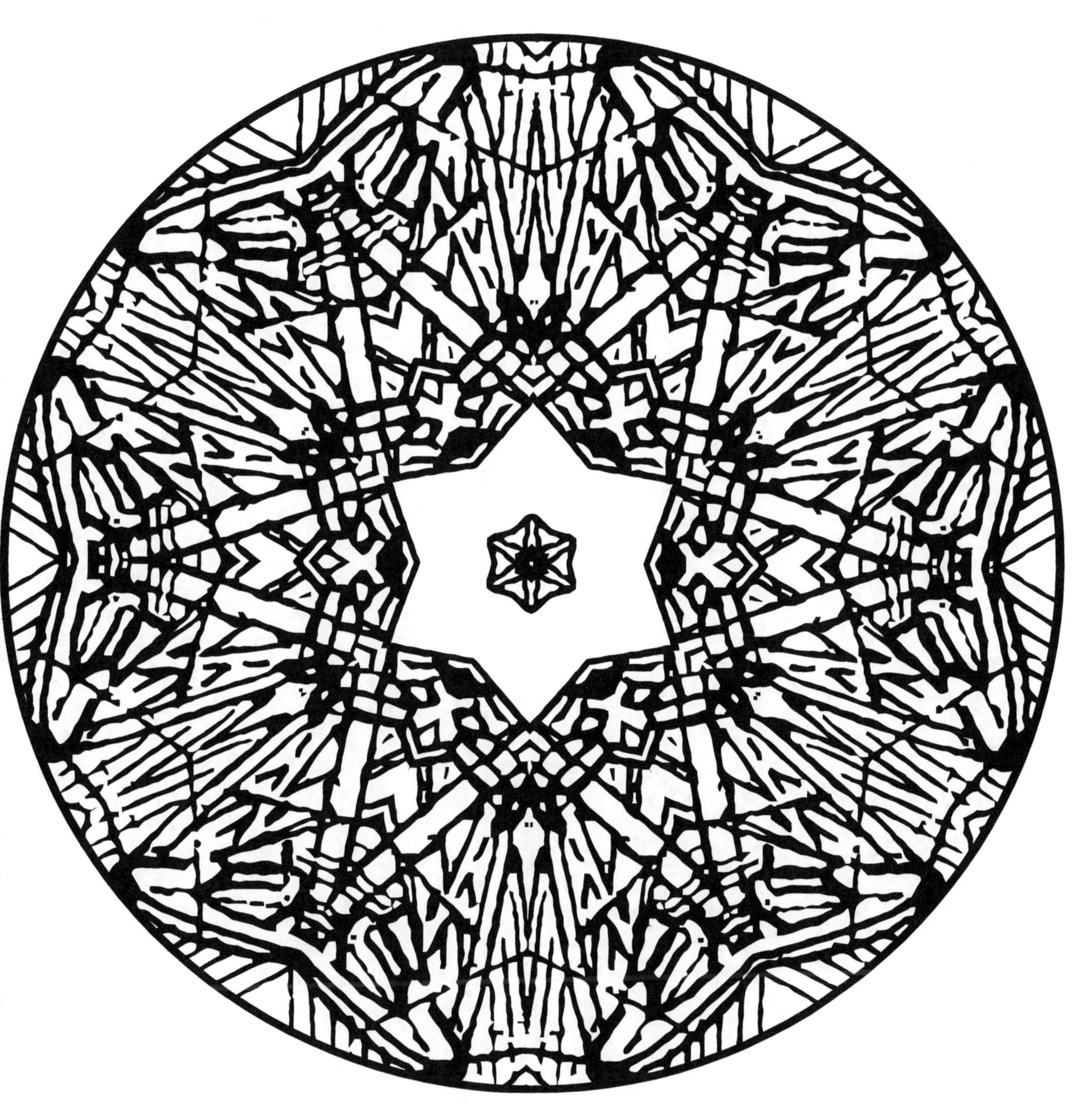

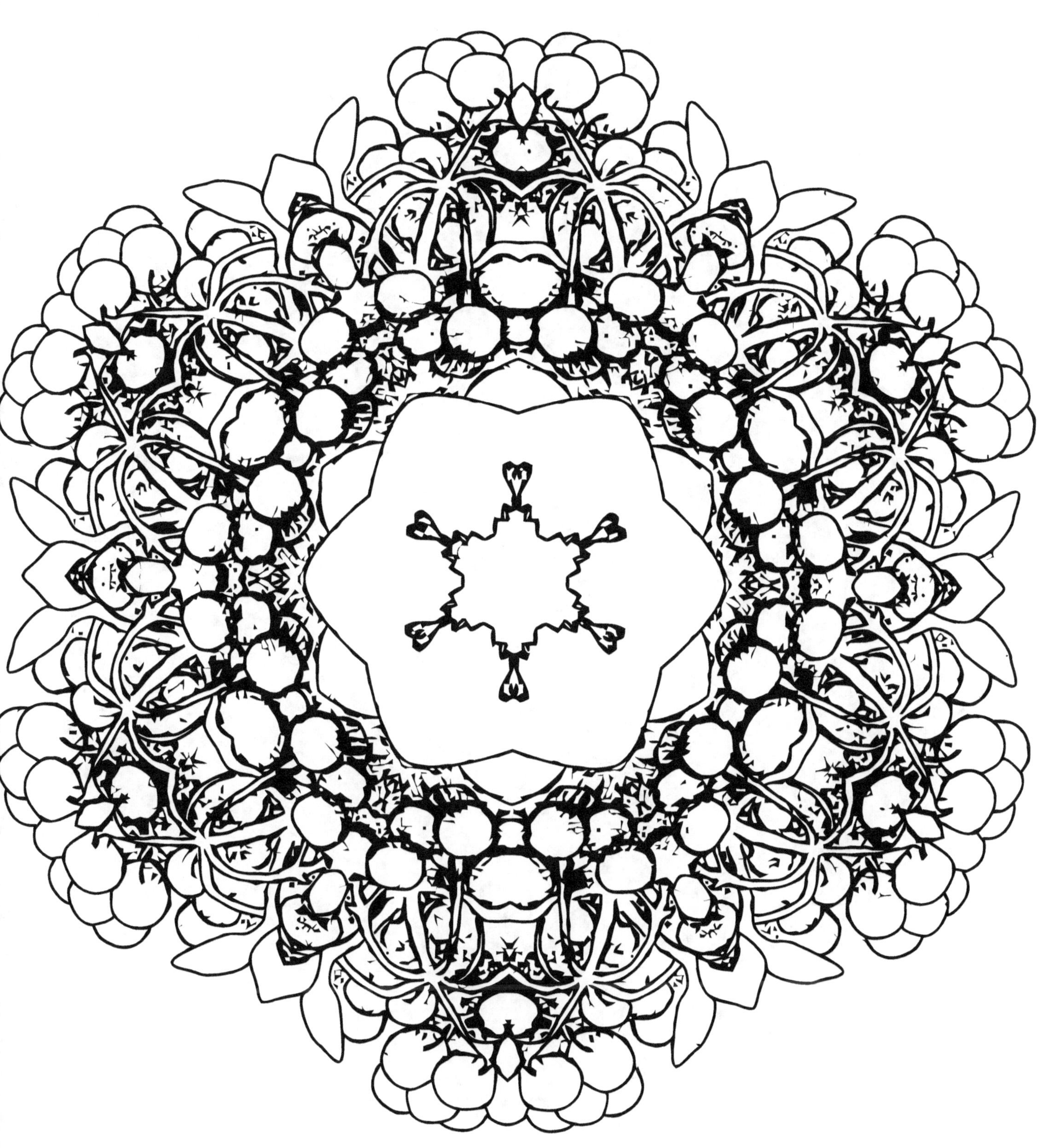

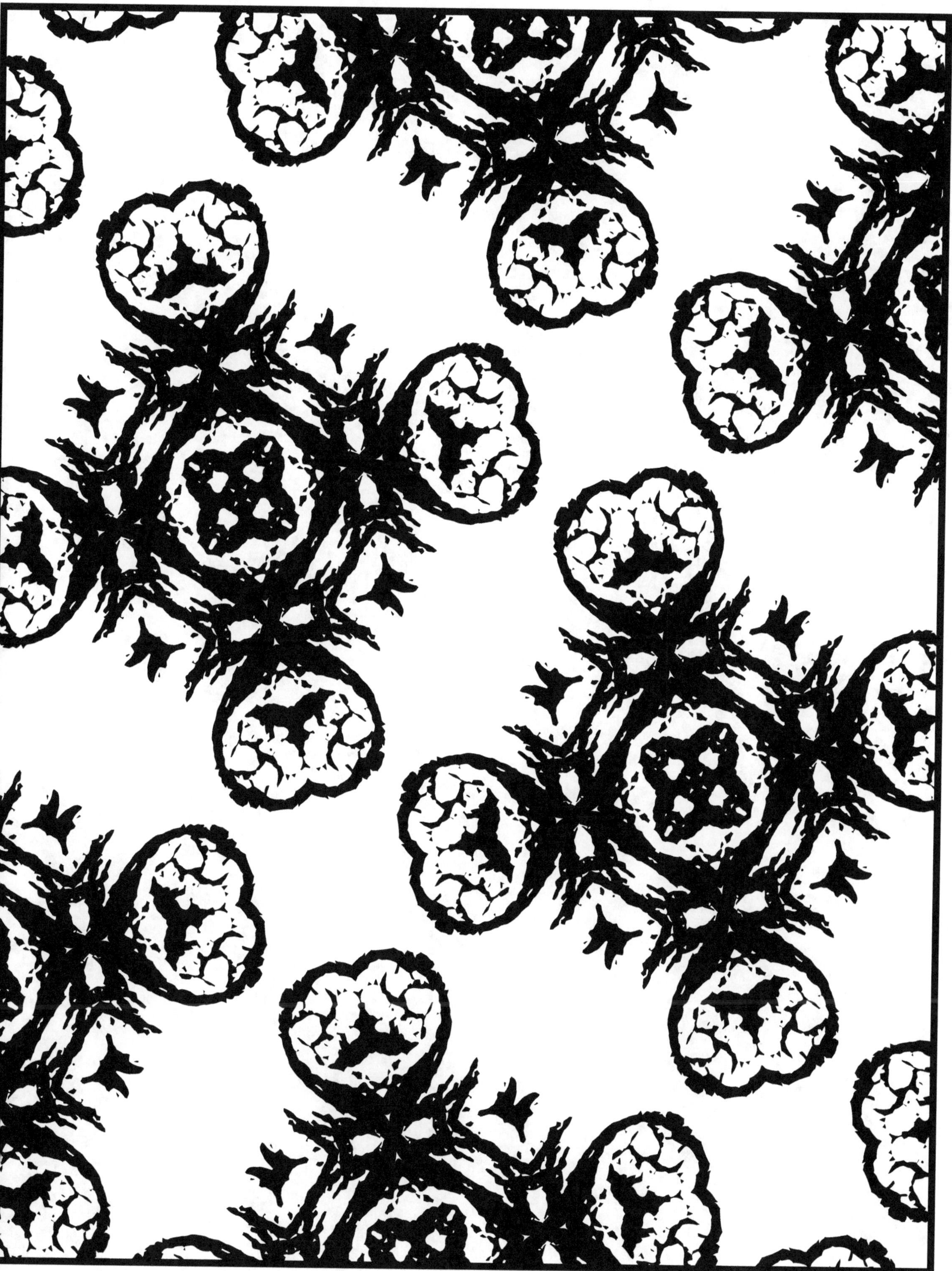

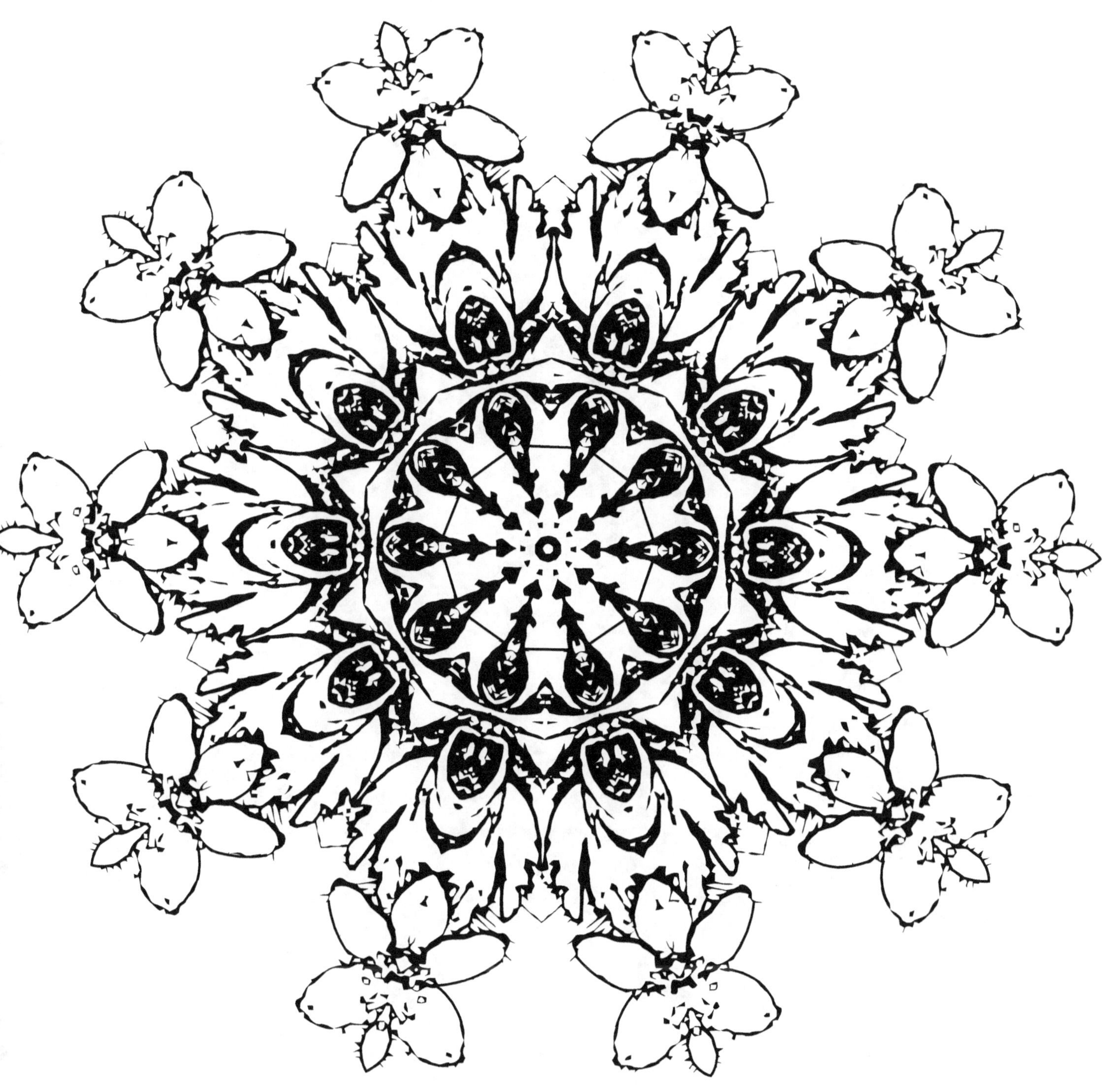

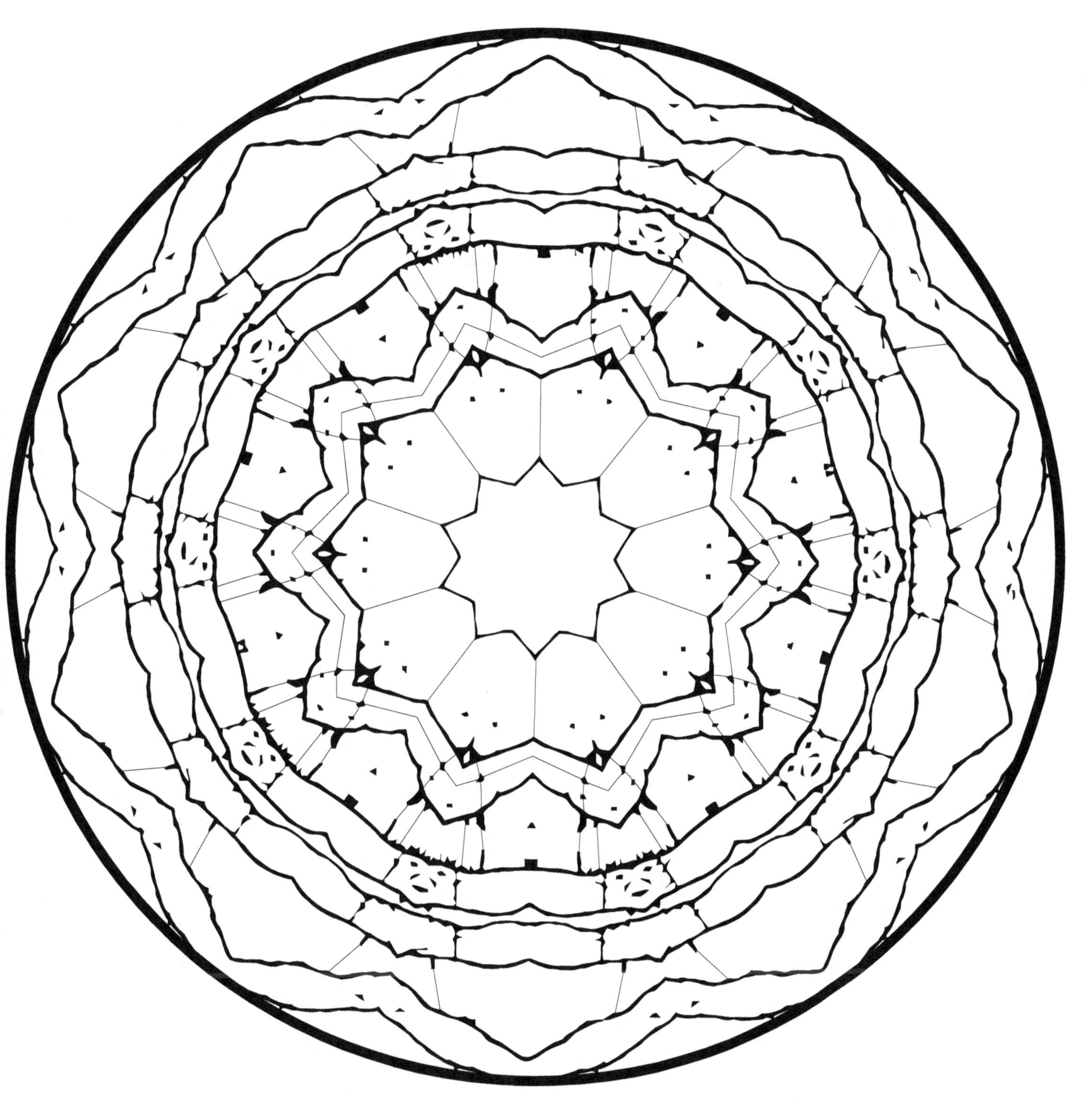

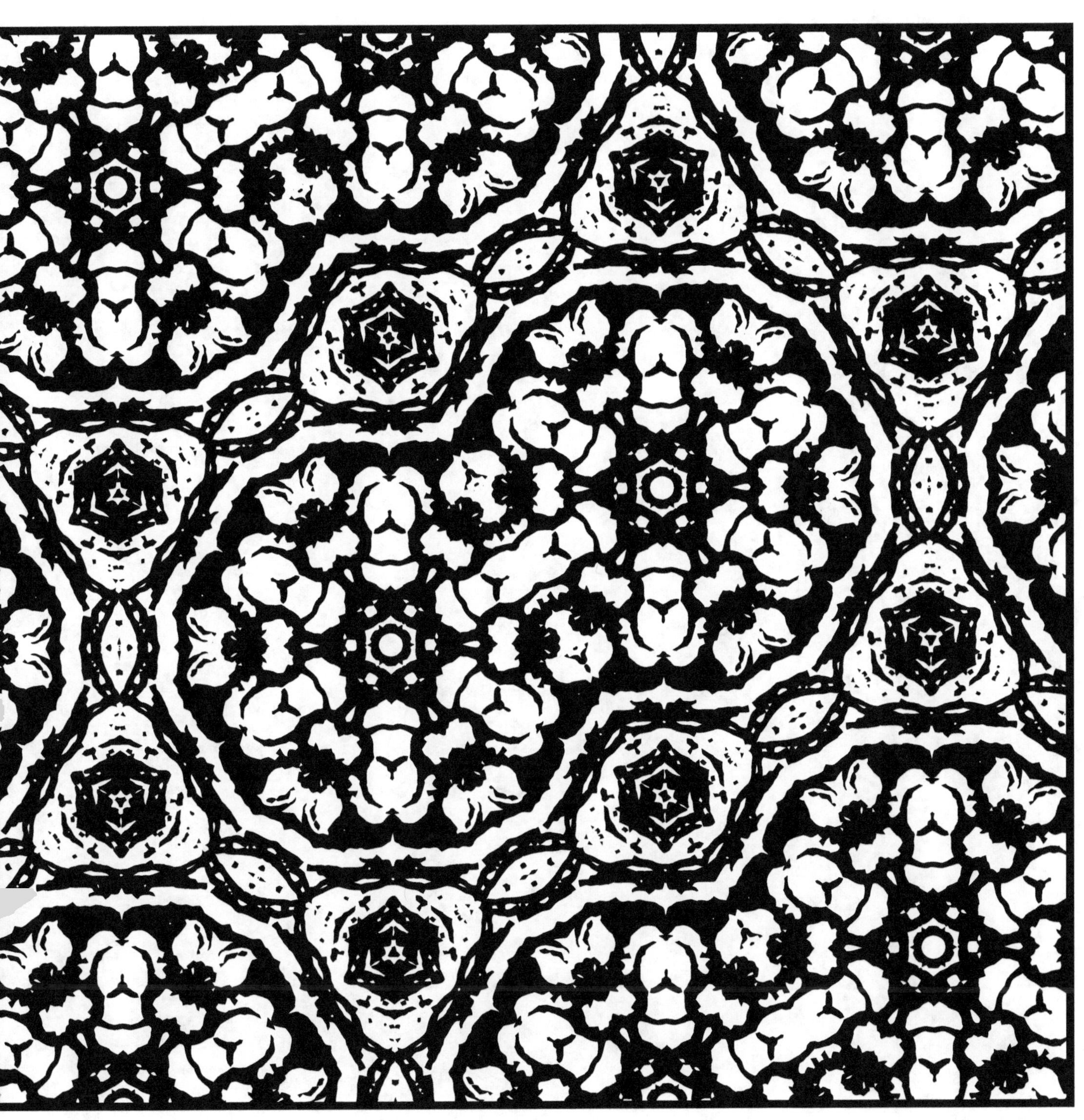

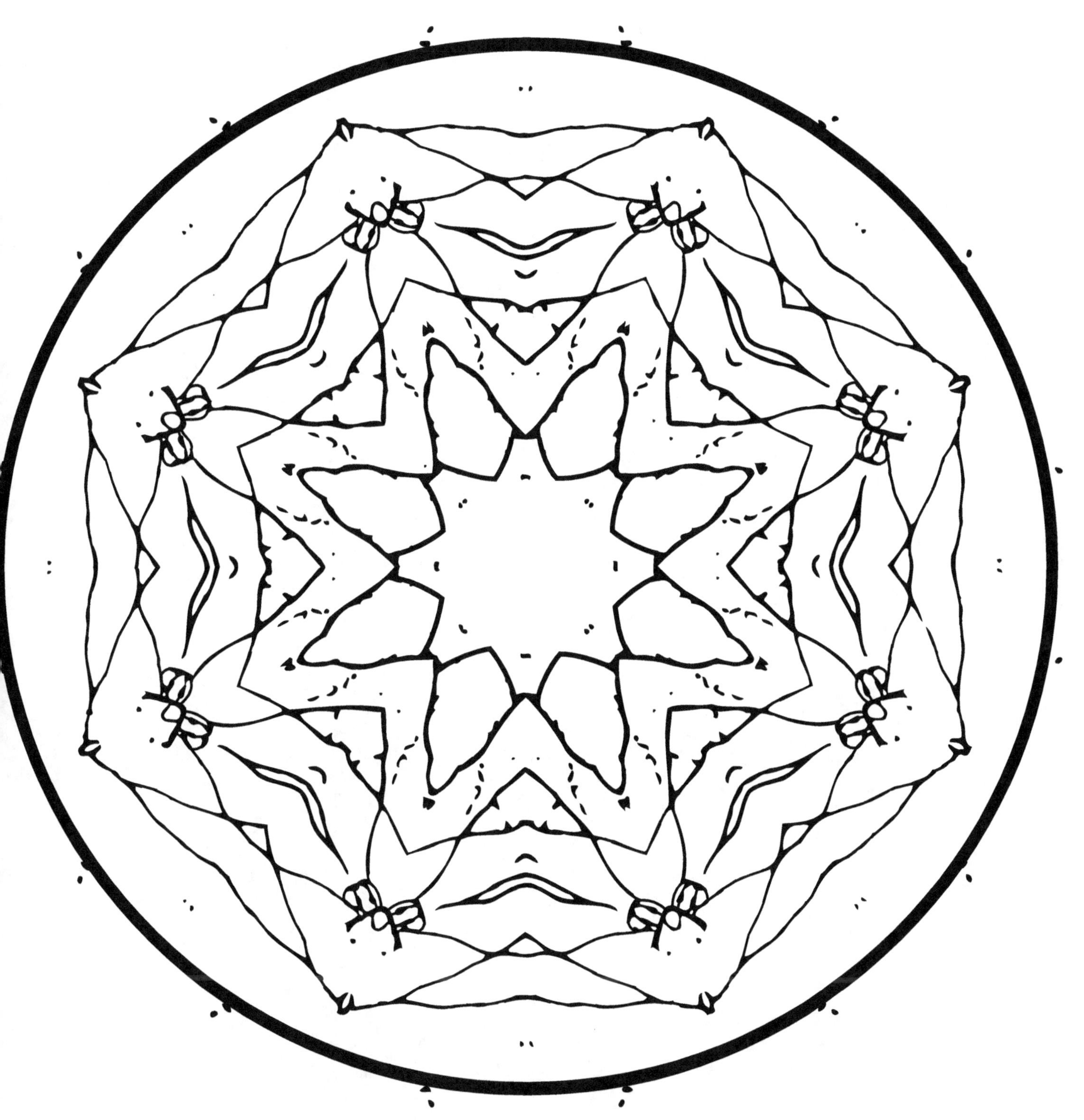

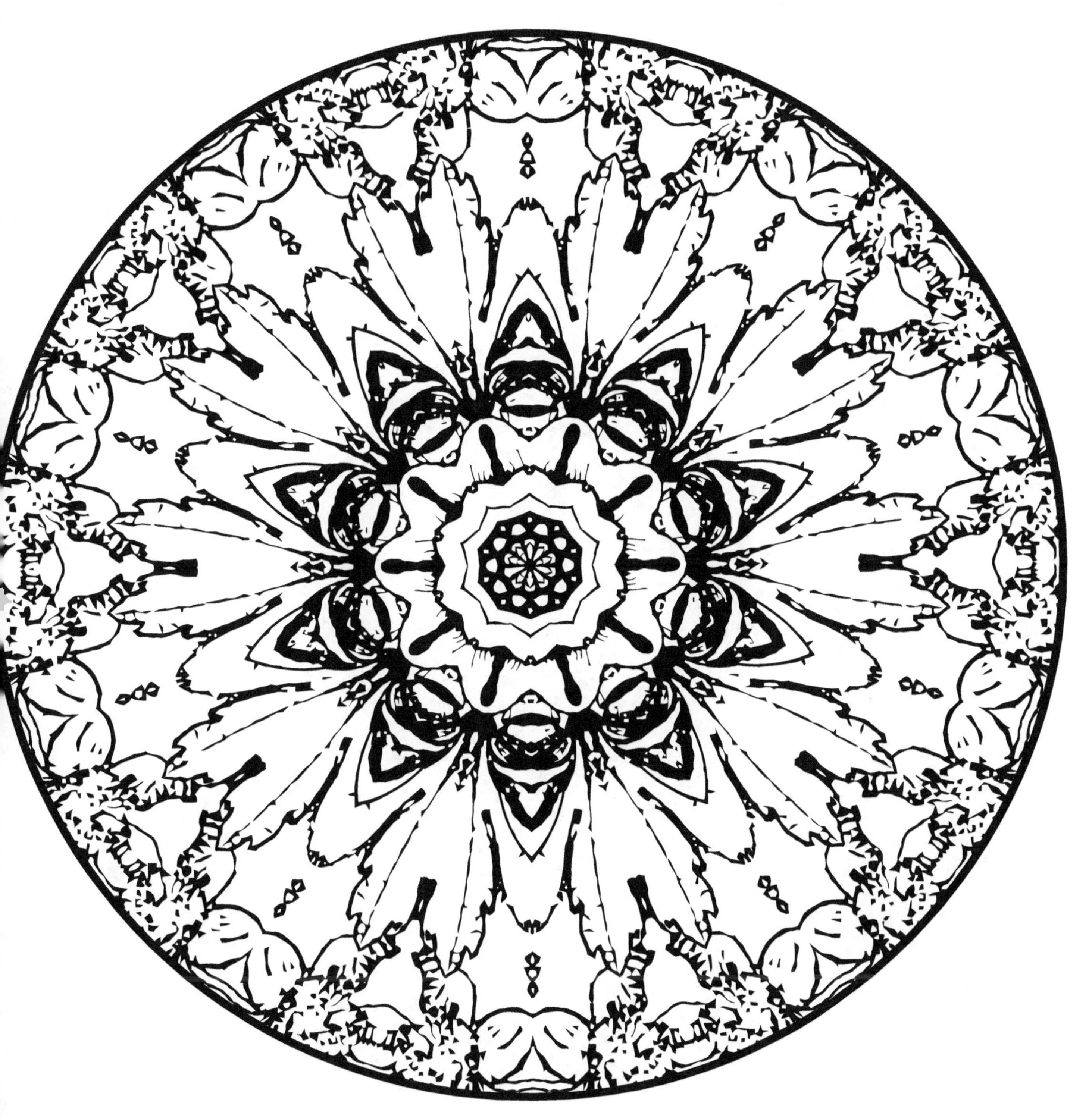

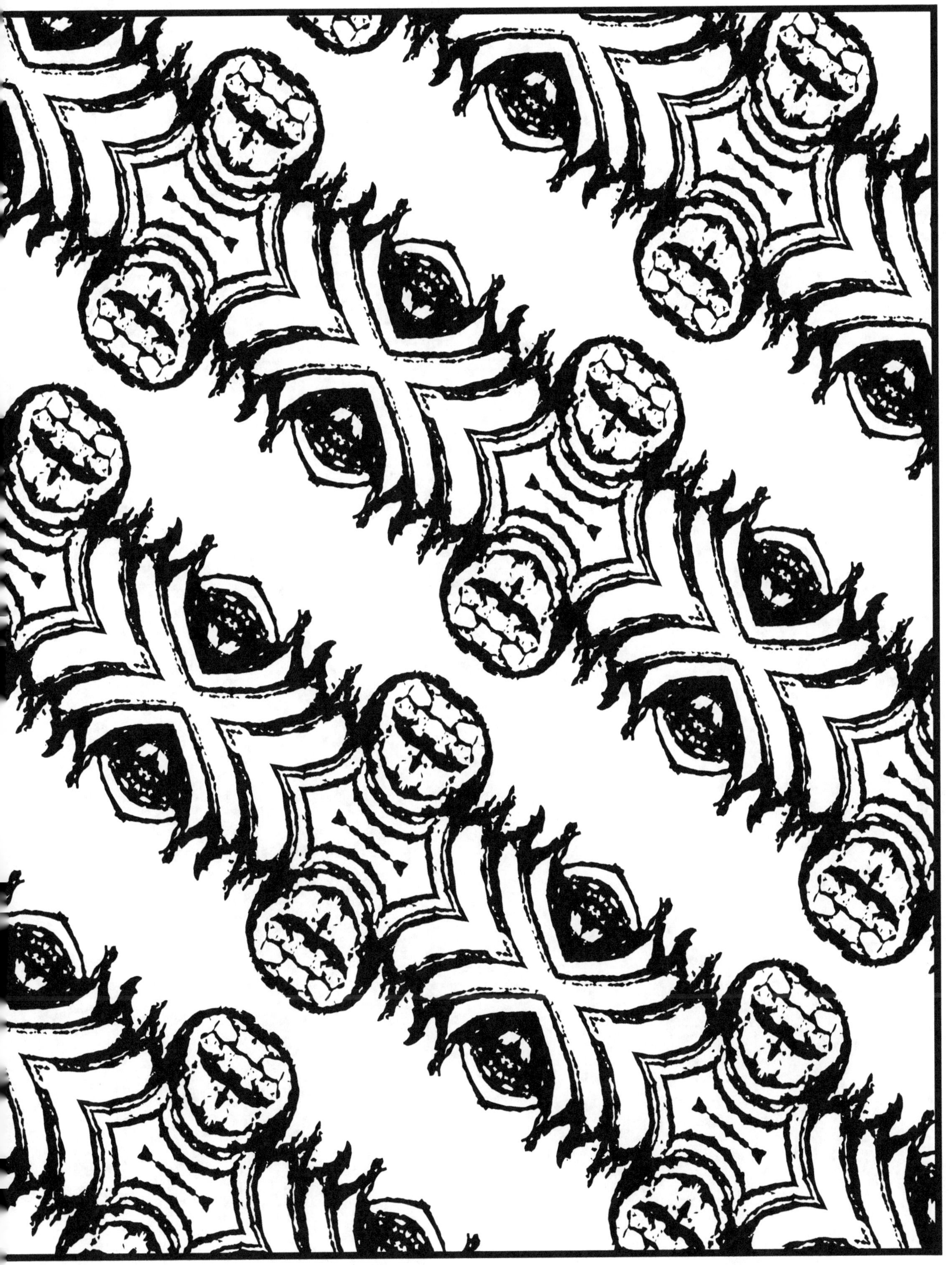

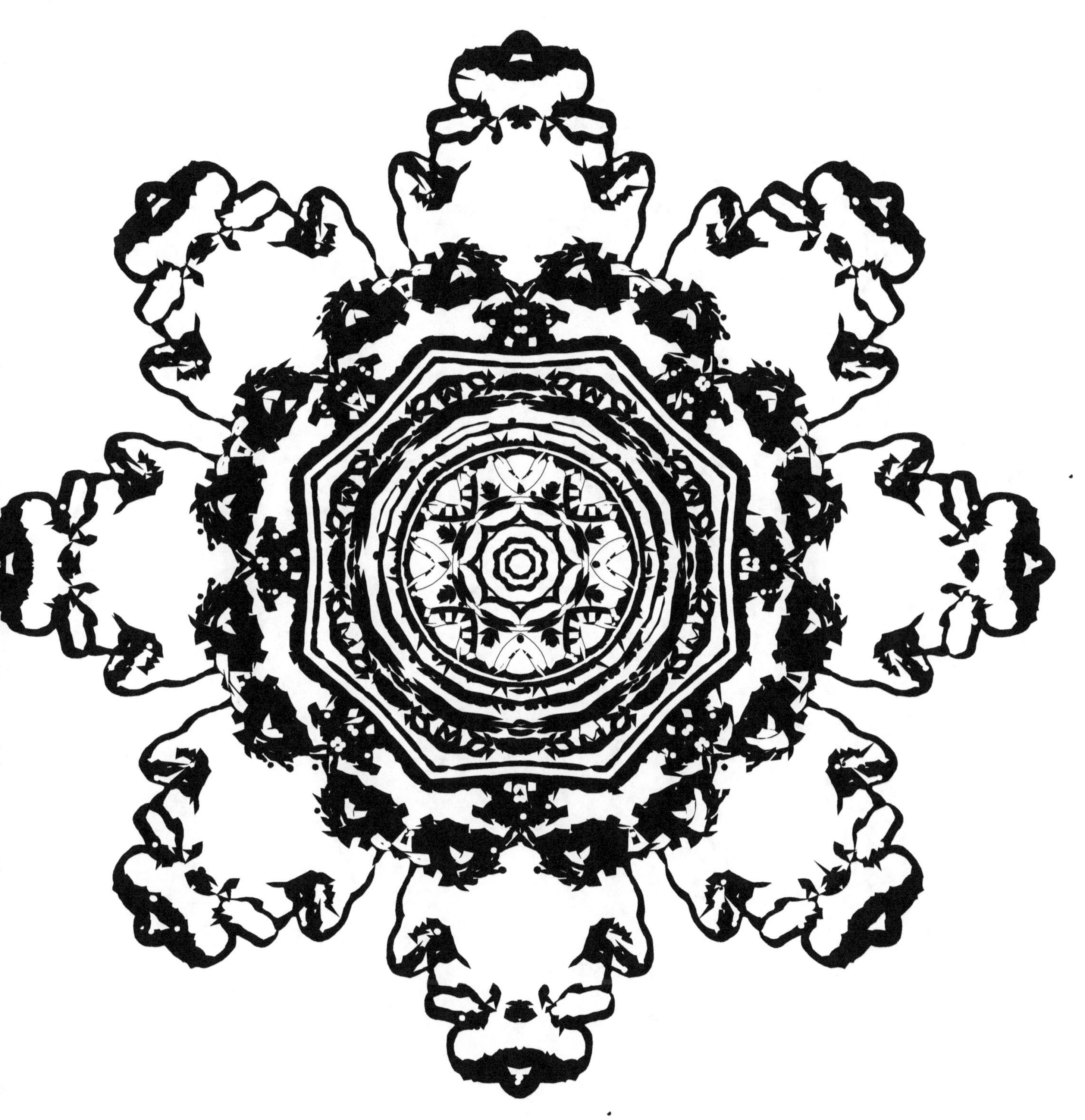

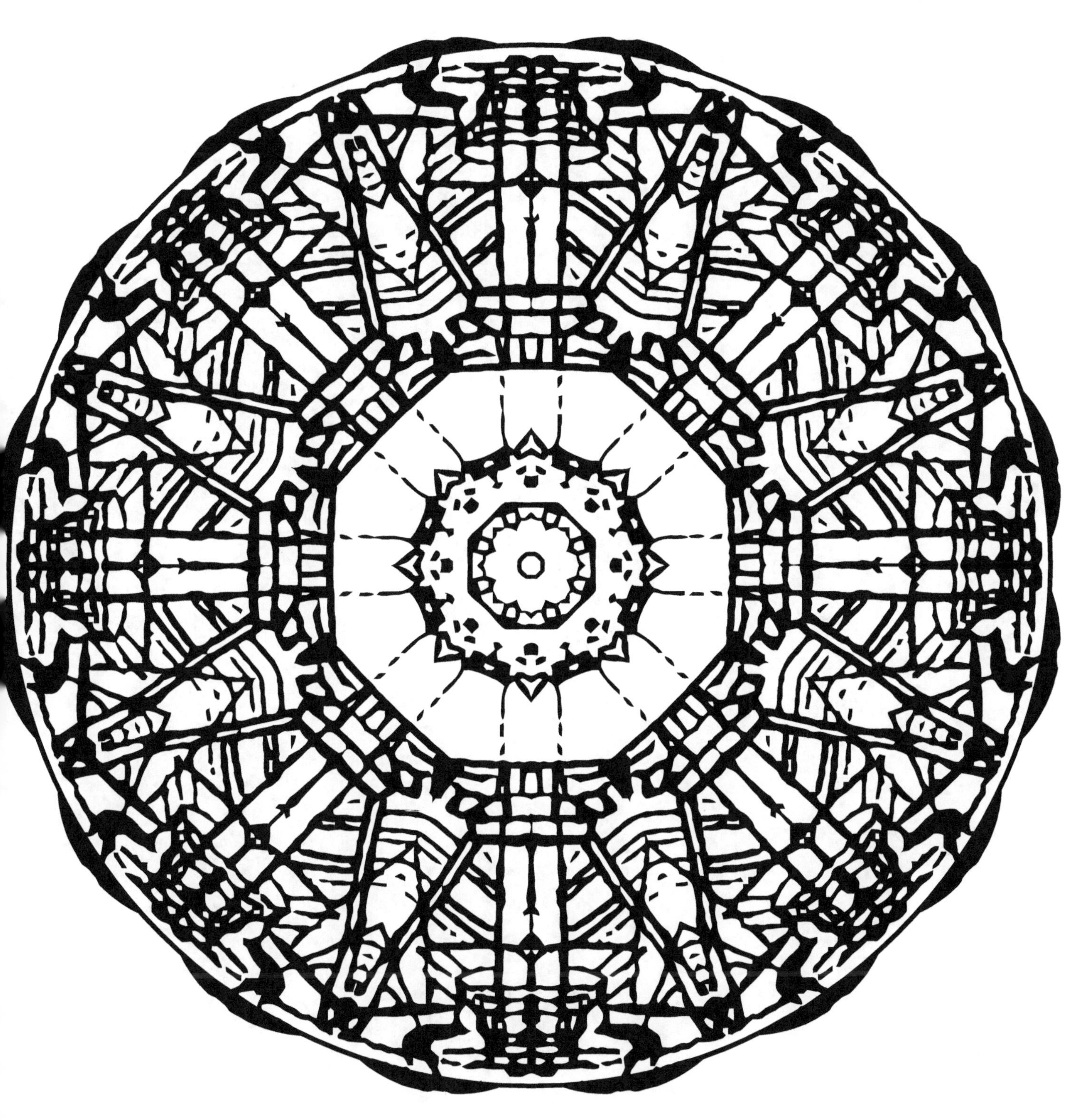

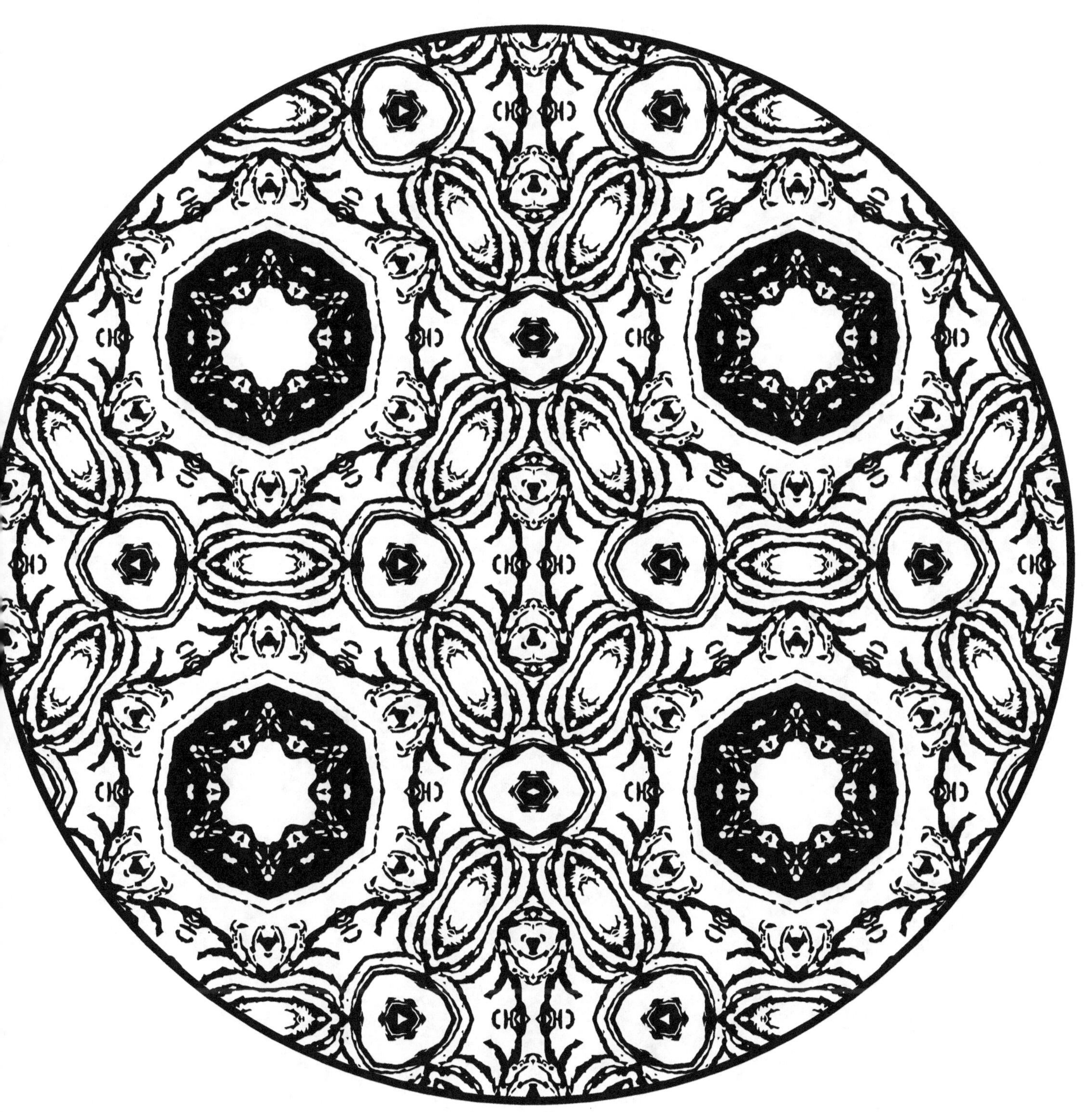

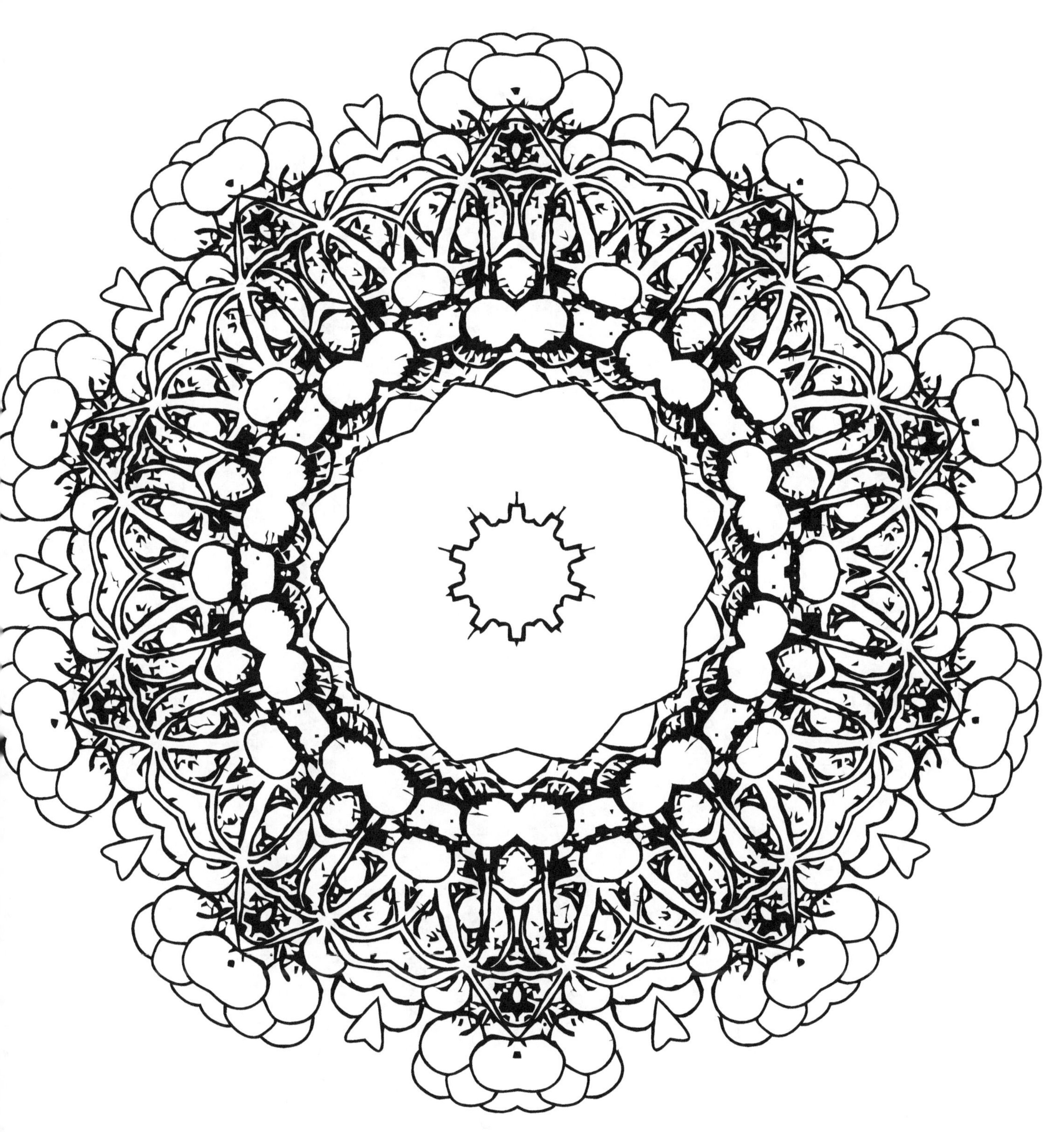

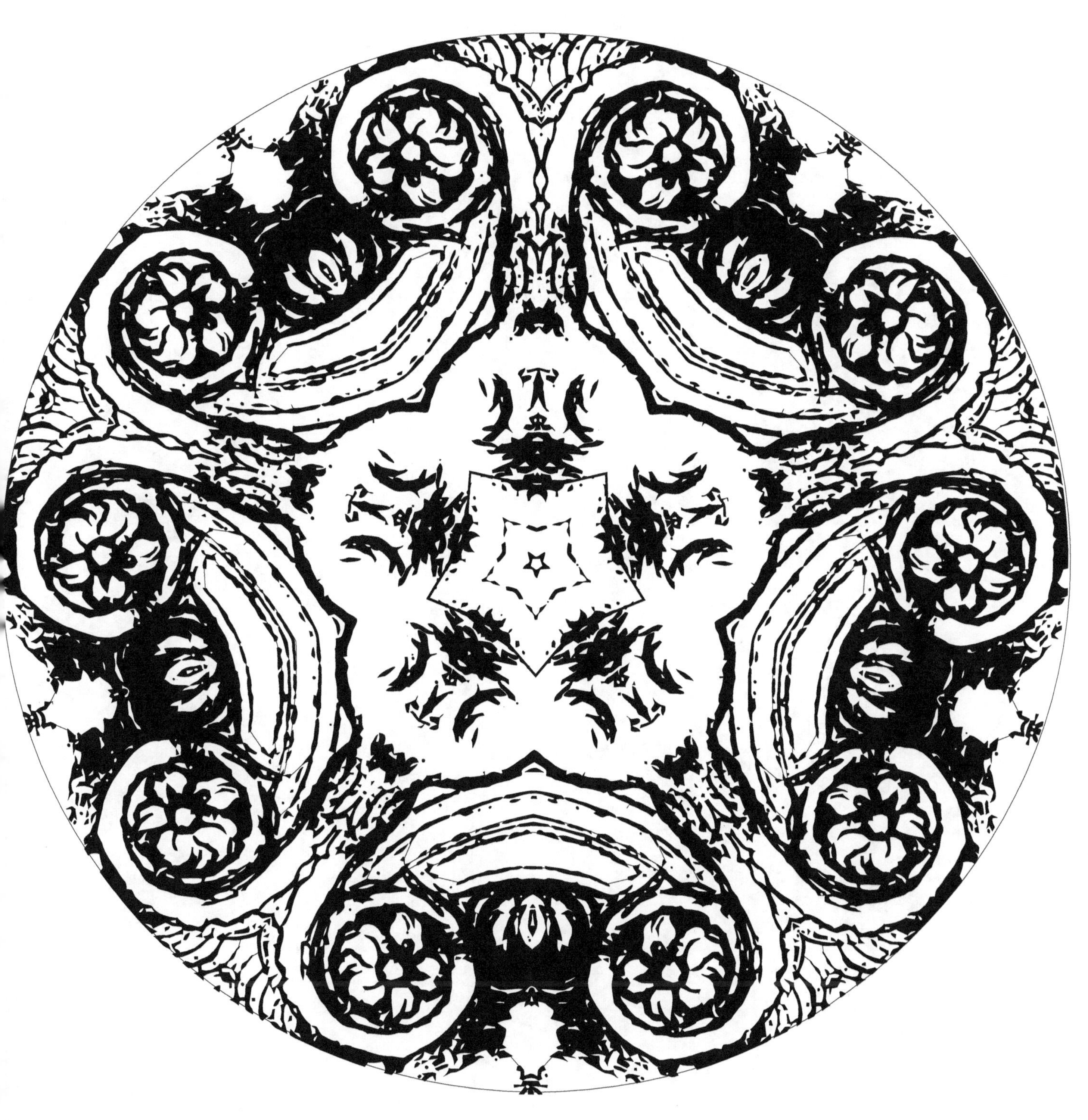

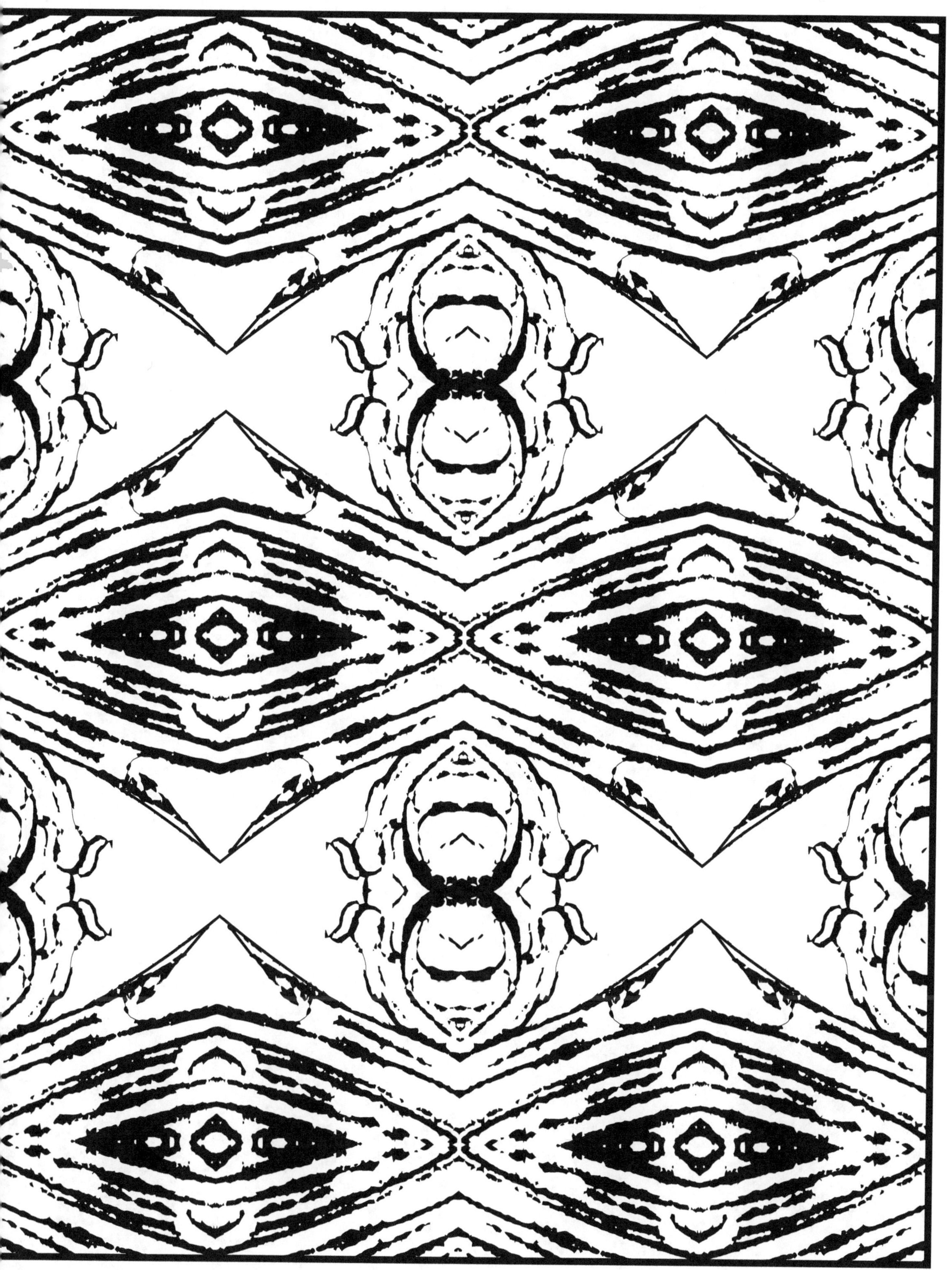

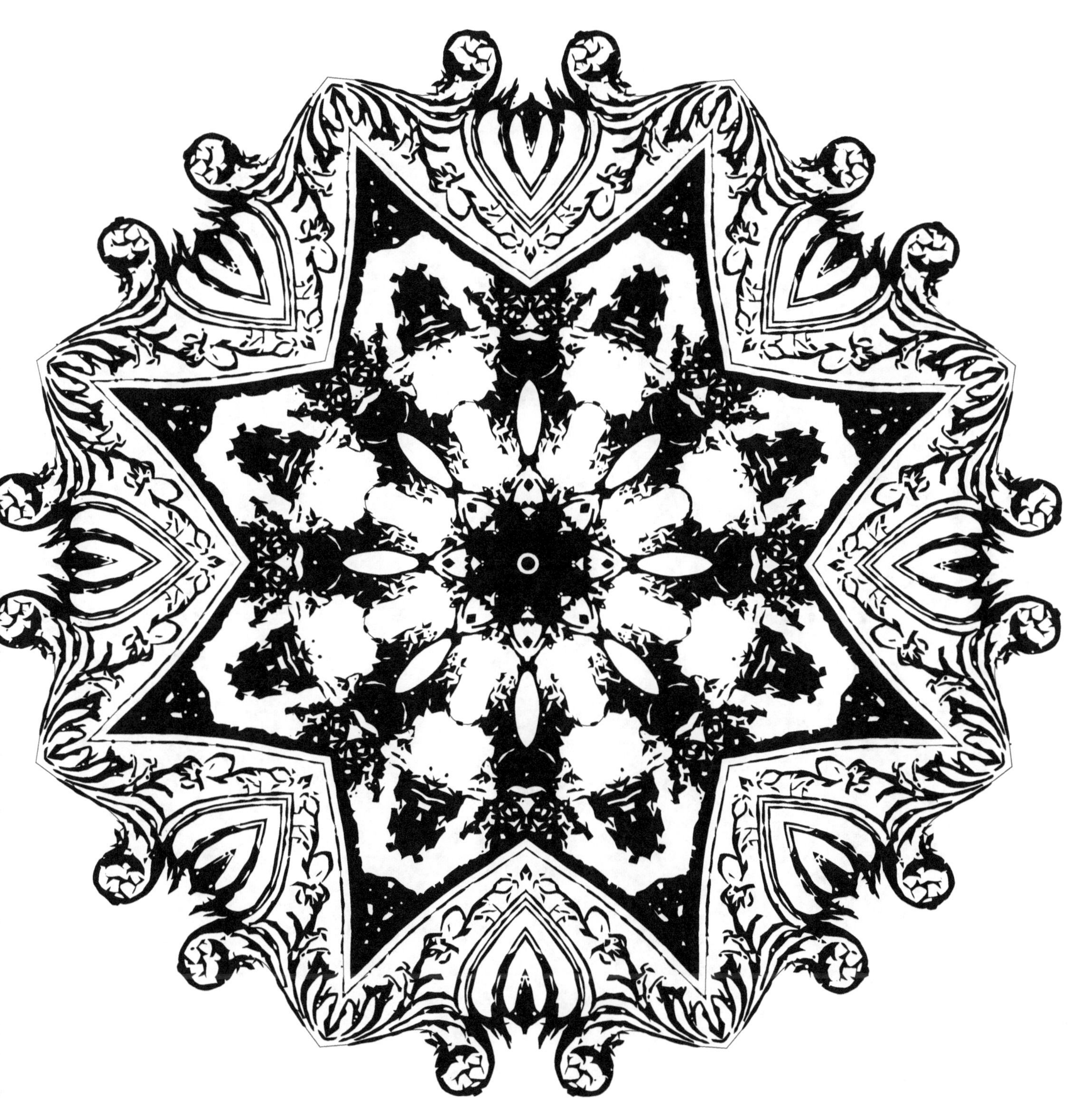

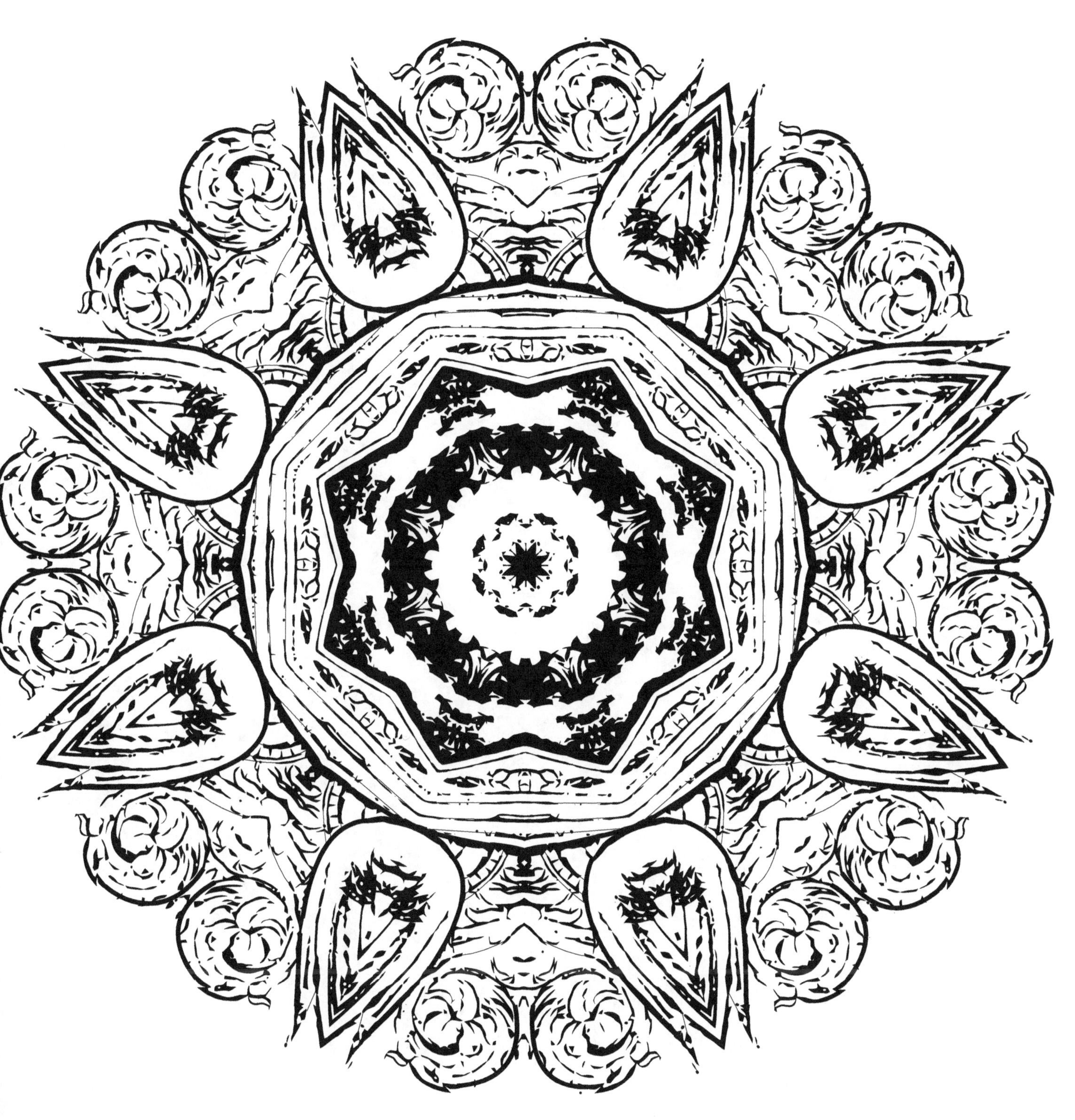

A•B•O•U•T
COLORING
& MANDALAS

FOR EVERYONE REGARDLESS OF SKILL

CREATIVITY AND PEACEFULNESS BOTH TAKE PRACTICE DO BOTH AT ONCE

COLORING

CREATIVE, CALMING AND FUN
UNIQUE EVERY TIME, NO TWO ALIKE
AS GENERAL OR AS DETAILED AS YOU LIKE
THERE IS NO "WRONG WAY" TO COLOR

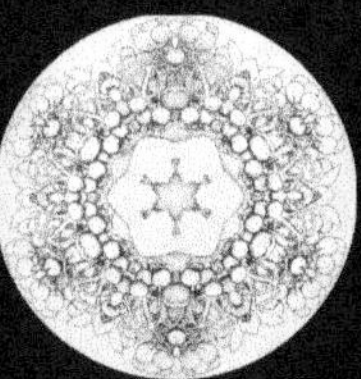

MANDALA

MEANS "THE UNIVERSE"
ALSO KNOWN AS A "HEALING CIRCLE"
THEY HAVE BEEN SYMBOLIC, ABSTRACT, FREEFORM AND USED AS A MEDITATION AID

MANDALAS HAVE BEEN CREATED IN MANY WAYS, AS A SYMBOL OF IMPERMANENCE USING SAND, RICE, STONES, AND CRYSTALS ARRANGED ON THE GROUND

A•B•O•U•T
MASTERPEACE
BOOKS

MINUTES OR HOURS YOU ALWAYS HAVE ENOUGH TIME & SKILL TO ENJOY COLORING

ANYTIME IS A GOOD TIME TO ENJOY THE BENEFITS OF SOME PEACE

The art work of the masters inspire us. Yet some shy away from art and being creative, seeing it as too time consuming to acquire skill. We were inspired to create these images, patterns and instructions so anyone who felt the urge to could experience the benefits of coloring..... having fun while mastering peace

VISIT US ONLINE FOR EXCLUSIVE COLORING DOWNLOADS AND OFFERS

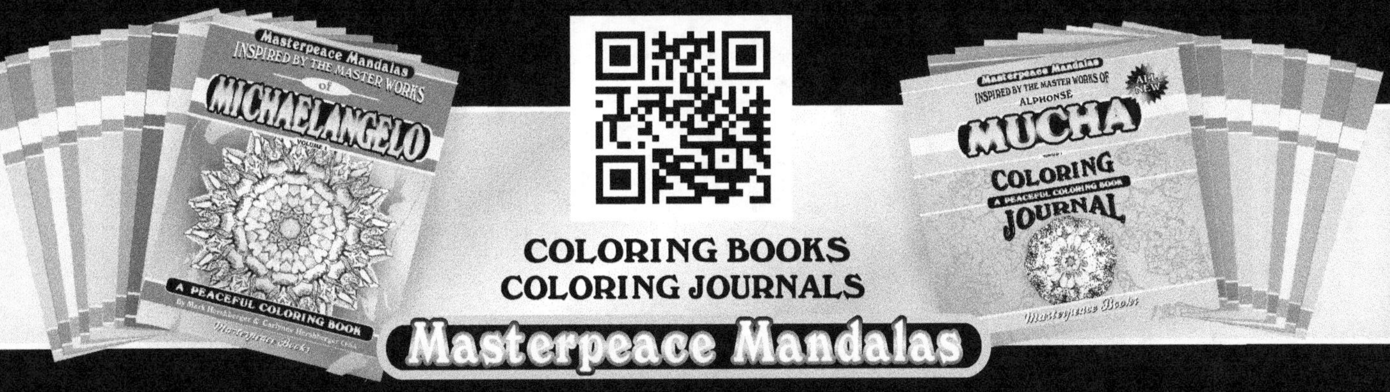

ABOUT THE AUTHORS

Mark Hershberger and Carlynne Hershberger CPSA

Mark and Carlynne, artists, living in central Florida where they met. Mark is an award winning commercial artist, fine artist and sculptor - Carlynne is an award winning fine artist, author, instructor and a signature member of the Colored Pencil Society of America - CPSA

WWW. MASTERPEACEBOOKS. COM

WOULD ENJOY HEARING WHAT YOU LIKED ABOUT OUR BOOKS - WE LOVE MAKING THEM AND WE WOULD LOVE TO HEAR WHAT YOU THINK

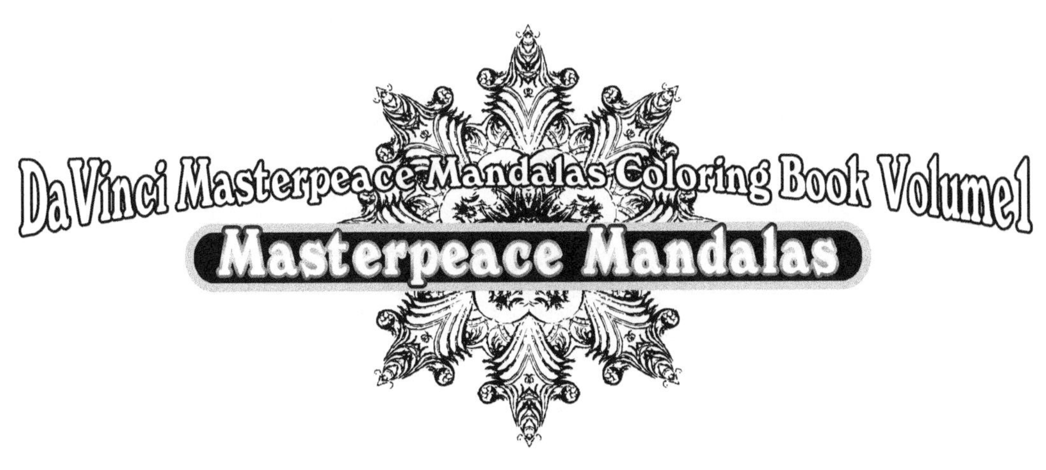

www.ingramcontent.com/pod-product-compliance
Lightning Source LLC
LaVergne TN
LVHW080328110826
845155LV00026B/215

* 9 7 8 1 9 4 4 3 8 1 0 0 4 *